THE OBEDIENT DOG

6 120164 7 104566

THE OBEDIENT DOG
Training for Obedience Classes, Working Trials and Agility Tests

JOHN HOLMES

Photographs by Sally Anne Thompson

POPULAR DOGS
London Melbourne Auckland Johannesburg

Popular Dogs Publishing Co. Ltd

An imprint of Century Hutchinson Ltd

Brookmount House, 62–65 Chandos Place,
Covent Garden, London WC2N 4NW

Century Hutchinson Australia (Pty) Ltd
PO Box 496, 16–22 Church Street, Hawthorn, Melbourne, Victoria 3122

Century Hutchinson New Zealand Limited
191 Archers Road, Po Box 40-086, Glenfield, Auckland 10

Century Hutchinson South Africa (Pty) Ltd
PO Box 337, Bergvlei 2012, South Africa

First published 1975
Revised editions 1977, 1980, 1985
Reprinted 1987

Set in Baskerville by BookEns, Saffron Walden, Essex

Printed and bound in Great Britain by Anchor Brendon Ltd, Tiptree, Essex

ISBN 0 09 159331 2

CONTENTS

ILLUSTRATIONS

All the photographs are of the author's own dogs

Author's Introduction

As THE title implies, my first object in writing this book is to help those who want an obedient dog. My second is to help those who aspire to winning prizes in Obedience Classes, Working Trials and Agility Tests. It may surprise some people to learn that these are not always synonymous. I have known several top winning dogs which were very disobedient when away from the confines of the obedience ring or training class. To me this is deplorable and I make no apologies for regarding an obedient dog as the prime objective.

Some books claim to cover fully every aspect of training and indeed some even claim to cover every aspect of dog owning. Anyone who believes that all aspects of training can be dealt with in one book knows very little about dogs. In my book *The Family Dog* I devote about half of the text to understanding instincts, temperament and general mentality of the dog before I give any advice on training. I have not done that in this book. Not because I now regard it as unimportant – far from it! It is because I want to deal fully with each and every exercise in the Obedience and Trials schedules and lack of space prevents me dealing fully with all the other aspects. I believe that the reason why some top winning dogs are not obedient is because their trainers lack a basic knowledge of canine mentality. Expert as they are at teaching a dog to sit, stand and do many other completely negative exercises they don't really understand what makes a dog tick.

I mention this because I have met a lot of people who have been given advice by instructors at training classes which was really quite frightening. And they have assumed that, because the advice came from someone who instructed at classes and had won in competitions, it automatically must be sound. Not everyone is as fortunate as I was when I first started in obedience. My first instructors at classes were George Sly and Bob and Audrey Montgomery, all well-known professional trainers with vast experience of training all sorts of dogs.

For longer than anyone knows, man has bred dogs for many and varied purposes, all of which involved the dog in actually doing something. Dogs worked sheep, retrieved game, coursed hares, killed rats and did a whole lot of other jobs. But at about the end of the last century man started breeding dogs as things of beauty with no thought of working ability. This fact, combined with the complete and radical change in our way of life, means that today only a tiny proportion of dogs ever have the opportunity to work. Hence we have dogs bred for hundreds, sometimes thousands, of years to do a job of work suddenly deprived of the opportunity to do anything. One result is the many neurotic and mentally unbalanced dogs we see all around us.

Now it is easy to say to a sheedog owner 'Let him work sheep' or to a gundog owner 'Let him work to the gun'. It is easy to say it but only possible for a small minority of dog owners to put it into practice. Like his owner, the present-day dog lives under unnatural conditions but he still has an active and very natural mind. So much is written about the necessity for physical exercise in the dog and so little about the equally important mental exercise. We hear a lot about physical cruelty – but nothing about mental cruelty. Indeed it is often the sentimental owner, the one who makes most noise about cruelty to animals, who causes untold suffering to his or her dog by failing to provide it with any opportunity to use its fertile brain. Few people are able to provide their dog with any work but anyone who has time to keep a dog has time to provide it with some artificial mental exercise. Properly carried out, obedience training is one of the best and easiest ways of doing this, though by no means the only one.

Generally speaking the obedient dog is much happier than the disobedient one. He leads a much fuller life because he can be taken places where his disobedient friend would create chaos; he can be allowed to run free where the disobedient dog would have to be kept on a lead and he will be popular with friends who visit you. It is astonishing how many owners with problem dogs when they appeal for help say 'We are losing all our friends!'

That is only one of the reasons why the owners of obedient dogs derive a great deal more pleasure from their animals than the owners of disobedient ones. Man and dog still retain many of their natural instincts and both derive the greatest pleasures in life through following them – even if they do sometimes lead to trouble! One of man's less dangerous instincts is his desire for achievement. A great deal of satisfaction can be obtained from training a dog. To transform an unruly dog into an obedient servant and loyal companion is a very satisfying experience indeed. And one has the pleasure of the resultant companionship on top of that.

To some people there is little satisfaction in achieving something without letting the world know about it. Call it the competitive spirit, one-upmanship, keeping up with the Joneses or what you like; it is certainly one of the strongest driving forces affecting mankind. It drives brave men to sail round the world or climb Mount Everest and the less brave to write books or train dogs for competitions! Without the desire to do some things a little bit better than the next man (or woman) life would become very dull indeed.

Another very good reason for competitions of all sorts is to demonstrate to the uninitiated the benefits to be derived from that particular sport. This is more important in dog training than ever before. On reading over this book I was surprised to find that in the original script I advised those in search of distractions not to 'make their dogs do Sits and Downs in chain stores and such like places.' That was less than ten years ago but today all such like places are plastered with NO DOGS signs. Even the good old British pub, once a mecca for dog owners with their dogs, very often has such a notice displayed.

Ten years ago I would not have believed that a strong anti-dog movement could develop in this country. But it has. And very dangerous it is too; with propaganda designed to terrify those who know nothing about dogs. The information on which this propaganda is based is usually very debatable and sometimes quite false. We cannot hope to convert the antis, most of whom are quite vicious, with huge chips on their shoulders. But we can influence those who might be swayed by their propaganda. Dog sports of all kinds help to show how well trained dogs behave. They also show how much pleasure is to be derived from owning such a dog. And I hope they show that those who train dogs are much more reasonable and nicer people than those who would have them exterminated.

Some people may wonder why, when I advocate competitive obedience as a hobby, I no longer compete myself. The answer lies in the fact that I am one of those fortunate people who has been able to turn a hobby into a career. Exasperating as it is at times, training dogs for film work can be very satisfying indeed – and it provides some money to feed the said dogs! But while the first essential in a competition dog is that he should concentrate on his handler and 'jump to it' when given a command, the first essential in a film dog is that he does neither of these things. This means that the two types of training just don't mix.

If at times I appear to be over-critical of some of the goings-on in obedience it is worth remembering that the onlooker sees most of the game. Especially if he has himself taken part in that game in the past. My criticisms are intended to be constructive and are certainly not intended to put people off obedience training. I have not forgotten that it was Obedience Classes and Competititions which set me on the way to training dogs professionally. And I first met my wife when she came to classes at which I was instructing!

I should like to emphasize that any criticisms I make are entirely my own opinion. Just because they are printed in a book does not make them any more valuable than many other opinions. And that applies to my advice on training just as much as to any remarks I make about rules and regulations. When I read a book I never believe it all at its face value. What I read I regard as the opinion of the author. I compare it with my own views on the subject and, if possible, with the views of other people – and then I form my own opinion. And that is what I hope my readers will do.

My first book was compiled and edited by the late Macdonald Daly from a series of articles I wrote for *Our Dogs* in the immediate post-war years. When it went out of print I wrote *Obedience Training for Dogs* (1961) using some of the original material. And when that book went out of print I wrote *The Obedient Dog* to replace it; and again I was able to use some of the material from the previous book. To me it is very significant that some of what I said nearly forty years ago is still relevant. It is not so surprising, however, when one remembers that, although times have changed a lot and people have changed too, dogs have changed hardly at all.

Indeed some of the things I said in those articles apply today far more than they did then. I was constantly harping on about the danger of obedience training becoming an end in itself – winning prizes in the ring – instead of a means to an end – a better-trained dog. It is obvious that my warnings have gone unheeded. We even have enthusiasts who talk of obedience-trained dogs as working dogs, thereby bringing upon their heads the ridicule of all those who work dogs. Many of today's most successful competitors can only be described as obsessed with winning prizes. They turn dogs into brainwashed automatons and themselves behave in a completely unnatural manner which makes them the laughing stock of many onlookers.

Obedience training to the dog should be like drill to the soldier. It makes him more alert, more responsive to commands and, in short, more obedient. But it does not make him a good soldier. The smartest man on the parade ground is not of necessity the best soldier. In fact he may be quite useless as a soldier. And the Obedience Champion may be just as useless as a worker. Carried to extremes obedience training can completely kill initiative and the desire to work.

Of course, this book is not confined to training for Obedience Classes. More than half of it is devoted to Working Trials, in which the dog does have the opportunity to work. Here the obedience training is the means to the end, provided you have first of all found a dog capable of being trained for the work. There is no reason why a dog should not compete in both Obedience Classes and Working Trials, although it is rare to find one that excels at both. Perhaps just as rare is the owner who excels at training for both. This is probably the reason why there has always been a tendency to have two camps with the Obedience enthusiasts in one and the Trials enthusiasts in the other.

And now we have a third option which may well appeal to some people who are not too keen on either Obedience Classes or Working Trials. I am referring of course to the new sport of Agility Tests. These are more exciting for both dog and trainer than Obedience Classes and less time consuming than training for Working Trials with long tracking sessions. They also provide mental and physical exercise for both dog and handler.

One of the problems in writing a book of this sort is in deciding the 'running order' of the different exercises. As far as possible I have started with the simple exercises and gone on to the more difficult ones. But the dog can easily be learning several of these exercises at one and the same time.

It should of course be remembered that the Kennel Club publishes up-dated regulations every few years which may have minor, or even major, changes in the competition rules, and so the reader is probably best advised to check with the Kennel Club. Copies of the latest regulations are easily obtainable from them.

My main hope is that this book will help you, my reader, to have an obedient dog which works with you as a team in a natural and happy manner. If he does, both you and he will derive a lot of pleasure from each other. Prizes can then be regarded as a bonus rather than an essential.

1985   J.H.

I

Choosing a Dog for Training

Puppy or Adult – What is the Best Breed? – Dog or
Bitch – Finding the Right Dog

THIS is a book on training, but first things must come first and
one cannot train without a dog. And if you have hopes of any
success in any branch of dog training you don't just want a
dog, you want a dog trainable for the purpose you have in
mind. This I consider as important, if not more important,
than the training itself. It is possibly true to say that there are
more mediocre trainers who have been successful with good
dogs than there are good trainers who have been successful
with bad ones.

The three questions most commonly asked in this connection are 'Should I buy a puppy or an adult dog?' 'What is
the best breed to train?' and 'Should I have a dog or a bitch?'
Although not the most important questions, we shall start
with these three.

PUPPY OR ADULT

This is one of the few questions I answer differently now than
I would have done twenty years ago. At one time I always
advised people to start with a young adult dog in preference to
a puppy. But a good deal of scientific research has been done
on the mental development of dogs. Quite a number of
trainers, including myself, have studied these reports and
allied them to our own observations. It now seems fairly
certain that a dog's mental characteristics can be influenced
even before its eyes are open. What is quite certain is that the
treatment a puppy receives from weaning at six weeks will
influence its whole future behaviour. My wife has, in fact,

always believed this and is now in the enviable position of being able to say 'I told you so'.

I now feel that the chance of eventual success is probably greater if you start with a young puppy than if you start with an adult dog. The reason is not because the puppy will become more attached to you than an older dog. If you and the dog are compatible it will become attached at any age. Twice I have acquired German Shepherd Dogs at nine years old and both have become devoted to me. No, the reason you may be better with a puppy is because you should be able to ensure that it is brought up properly. You will also have a much better selection of young puppies to choose from compared with adults. And they won't have any bad habits, which is nearly always the case with adult dogs looking for new homes. Later on I shall deal with picking a puppy or adult for training.

WHAT IS THE BEST BREED?

To this I usually answer: 'No breed is best. It is the individual that matters.' This, however, is only partly true. Before answering the question one must decide what one wants to train the dog for. If you have ambitions to run in PD Trials there is little point in starting off with a Miniature Dachshund puppy! On the other hand, don't get the impression that the breeds most usually seen in trials are the only ones capable of being trained or that they are easier to train. It is interesting to note, and somewhat ironic, that the Airedale, the breed first used as guard dogs in World War I, is a popular police dog in Germany and Russia yet rarely used in this country. Speaking generally, the breeds which are best for training are those which have recently been used for working. Again speaking generally, these belong to the herding and gundog groups.

I have had great success with first crosses (not to be confused with mongrels) and only once had a failure. In all branches of livestock breeding except dogs it is an accepted fact that a first cross often produces the good qualities of both breeds. It has also been found that first crosses have what is known as hybrid vigour. And I believe this vigour to be mental as much as physical. This does not apply to mongrels and I would only have one if it had proved to have some outstanding qualities.

DOG OR BITCH

At one time the question of whether to keep a dog or a bitch required much more consideration than it does now. This is due to the fact that over the past twenty years much more has been learned about the effect of castrating dogs. I first brought this controversy out into the open in a column I wrote for *Our Dogs* for many years. I am, therefore, pleased to note that what I thought at the beginning has been proved correct. Practically all the arguments against castration are based on prejudice and/or ignorance. For many years all the dogs I have owned have been castrated except those I wanted for breeding. So far as training is concerned, a castrated dog is little different from a bitch.

I must however, warn against castration too soon. Some veterinary surgeons will advise castrating a puppy at four or five months old. Others will refuse to carry out the operation at all, saying that it will result in a creature devoid of character and liable to obesity. The fact is that dogs castrated before maturity are nearly all devoid of character and liable to obesity, but this does not apply to dogs castrated after maturity. Therefore the veterinary surgeons who refuse to operate are merely being guided by their own mistakes.

Apart from having owned and worked many castrated dogs (probably more than anyone in this country) I have made a careful study of the subject and have come to a number of definite conclusions.

Castration does not change a dog's character in relation to his human master. It does not weaken any of the useful instincts – hunting, retrieving, guarding or herding. It does weaken the sex instinct, which is only necessary in a stud dog and often conflicts with the useful instincts. Because it weakens the sex instinct it does in the case of some dominant males weaken the pack leader instinct. It can in fact turn an untrainable dog into a trainable one. For the same reason it can reduce the tendency to fight, especially if a bitch in season is around. But this only applies to the dominant dog which fights for supremacy. The habitual fighter which has developed a liking for fighting is unlikely to be improved by castration. Likewise the nervous fighter which gets its hackles up and goes rigid at the sight of any other dog is almost certain to do the same after he has been castrated.

There is some difference of opinion in the veterinary profession as to the best age to spay a bitch. However, it is generally agreed amongst those who have studied the subject (unfortunately that does not include all vets) that it is safer to wait until the bitch has been in season at least once. Spaying at three or four months, as is frequently done, often leads to obesity and other glandular problems.

Unlike the castrated dog, the spayed bitch does not change at all. The only advantage, therefore, is that she will not come in season and that, of course, can be a very great advantage.

FINDING THE RIGHT DOG

If you want a dog for a specific class of work the place you are most likely to find it is from a strain bred for that purpose. In both gundogs and sheepdogs one can be guided by the Trials record of the ancestry. If I buy a gundog puppy bred from a Field Trial strain I know that its ancestors retrieved, faced cover and water and were not gun-shy. If I buy a sheepdog puppy from a Trial strain I can expect it to have a strong 'eye' and a very strong (probably too strong) herding instinct. In either case I can expect the puppy to want to do the things I want it to do. The Guide Dogs for the Blind Association has for some years run their own breeding scheme. The percentage of failures from litters bred for the job is far lower than from those brought in.

So you might think that if you want to train a dog for obedience classes you should try to find one from an obedience strain. But I doubt if it is likely to be any easier to train than one from any other strain. Obedience tests are and always have been just as much a test of the trainer's ability as of the dog's natural trainability. For instance, it is possible for a dog to get consistently high marks for the retrieve although initially it was completely devoid of any natural inclination to retrieve.

Working Trials are slightly better and dogs bred from PD and TD strains should inherit some of the necessary characteristics to train for these purposes. But don't forget that a dog which is gun-shy and fails to stand up to the test of courage can qualify PD ex. and become a Working Trials Champion. I do not know that it has ever happened but the fact that the rules make it possible is surely ludicrous.

Here you must decide whether you want to go in for competitions only or whether you have ambitions to go on to Working Trials. I hope you will do both, but dogs which excel at both are the exception rather than the rule.

Obedience dogs fall roughly into two categories. On the one hand is the clinging, submissive dog ever anxious to respond to the slightest signal from its handler, but with no thought of ever doing anything of its own accord. On the other is the boisterous unruly dog which by constant repetition can, to a certain extent, be brainwashed into submission without losing its bounce and go. Neither requires a great deal of intelligence, which does not mean that no obedience dogs are intelligent.

Contrary to common belief, intelligence does not make a dog trainable. The majority of difficult and disobedient dogs are intelligent. Unfortunately they often end up with owners who show little sign of this quality!

It is a strong submissive instinct which makes a dog trainable. An instinct derived from the wild dog's instinct to obey a pack leader and in some cases strengthened by selective breeding over hundreds of years. The extreme example of this is the Border Collie, a breed that I have bred, trained and worked for longer than any other. And a breed which includes the stupidest dogs I have ever kept for any length of time. But they worked, and worked well. Why? Because the herding instinct was so strong it was almost a mania. They worked because they could not help it and it would be impossible to control this instinct if the submissive instinct were not equally strong.

Deprived of an outlet for this abnormal instinct these dogs quickly become frustrated and neurotic, and this is probably the worst of all breeds to keep as a pet. Provided with an alternative to herding they will enter into it with an enthusiasm amounting almost to a mania and the submissive instinct becomes even stronger. That is why they often do so well in the obedience ring. Having worked, and seen these dogs working, in the wide open spaces it is seldom that I enjoy seeing them in obedience competitions, even though I know they are often better cared for than their relatives on farms.

The prospective Working Trials dog should have a much steadier temperament. He will have some positive incentive to work instead of doing completely negative repetitive exercises. Many very good working dogs are slack on heel work but they cannot lose more than five marks on it. A successful Trial dog requires initiative and will have the opportunity to use his intelligence. He need not be quite so submissive. When I recall some of the top class PD dogs for which I have acted as criminal, that last remark is something of an understatement!

Don't conclude from what I have just said that intelligence does not matter. Although not always so easy to train, an intelligent dog can be taught a great deal more than a stupid one. It is also more enjoyable to train – and much more enjoyable to own. It really depends on how he uses his intelligence. He may use it to help you or he may use it to find ways of evading your wishes. Remember too that intelligence and temperament have nothing to do with each other. Many very shy, nervous dogs are exceptionally intelligent. Many very bold, fearless dogs are merely too 'dim' to be afraid.

Far more important than intelligence (and a point all too often overlooked) is that the dog and the trainer should have temperaments to suit each other. There are some who like a responsive dog, even if he is a bit soft and inclined to be 'touchy', and will get very good results from this type by coaxing and persuading. There are others who always like a hard dog, which has to have everything drummed into him and which couldn't care less if his handler does get a bit cross with him. Swop them round and you have two dogs and two handlers which, nine times out of ten, will never get anywhere at all.

The one canine temperament which I should never advise anyone to waste time on is the really shy, nervous one. I know that some have had amazing results from shy dogs, but the time spent taking them around and getting them accustomed to strange people and surroundings could be much more profitably spent at home training a dog with a good temperament. In any case a shy dog is always liable to let one down in a competition before the public.

How do we go about finding a puppy likely to grow into the sort of dog we want? The most important guide at this age is to be found in the pedigree. I don't mean that cherished piece of paper with all those illustrious names on it. I mean the dogs which go to make up the whole ancestry of the puppy in question. Only people who have been in a breed for some time know these dogs and my advice, therefore, is to seek the advice of such a person.

Of course, you may be able to see quite a lot of the puppy's relatives for yourself and you should make every effort to do so. And don't just go on what you see. If you fancy a dog at a Trial go and have a chat with the owner and try to find out as much as you can about the dog himself. The owner may say 'He's a good dog now but he was a cussed brute to start with. Even now he'll take advantage when he can.' He will no doubt say this with pride at having moulded this cussed brute into something which you admire. You may like to think of the same sort of satisfaction from one of his puppies.

But you may not be the sort of person who gets on with that sort of dog. Better for you the dog whose owner says 'He's never been a bit of trouble right from the start. Won't stand any harsh treatment but always tries to do what I want.'

If you are thinking of buying a puppy by a particular dog find out what you can about his forbears especially his dam. Over many years breeding many types of livestock I have found that all the best stud animals are from good dams. This view is shared by many stockmen more experienced than myself and it is interesting to note that Arabs will sell their good stallions but never their good mares.

Now let's move on to consider the dam of a prospective purchase which is even more important than the sire. It has been found that puppies removed from a bitch of bold temperament and fostered on a nervous bitch become nervous, while the remainder of the litter left with their own mother showed no sign of nervousness. This means that puppies from a nervous bitch are likely first of all to inherit that nervousness and then to acquire even more while still in the nest. The same applies to gun-shyness which is not always associated with nervousness. Puppies reared on a gun-shy bitch are more likely to be afraid of bangs than those reared on a bitch that is not gun-shy.

Of course, puppies do not inherit all the characteristics of their parents. The grandparents and great grandparents play an important part and indeed some characteristics (usually bad ones) can be handed down from much farther back than that. Nothing is more likely to bring disappointment than the assumption that a puppy will inherit the good points of both parents in equal proportions.

Small breeders with one or two bitches kept as companions are more likely to produce good training propositions than big kennels. The more 'humanizing' a puppy has in its early life, the better will it settle down when it leaves its mother. At one time it was considered bad for puppies to allow children to handle them, but, provided they don't hurt them, it definitely does good. If the bitch really is a member of the family she will not object to other members fondling the puppies. Many bitches will, in fact, proudly present their puppies for admiration.

Having found a litter of pups you fancy, the next step is obviously to pick the best puppy from the litter. Or at least the best one the breeder has for sale. Here the breeder is in a far better position than you to know how the pups are likely to turn out. It has been found by carefully controlled observation that the most adventurous puppy at birth remains the boldest for life. Few breeders have the time, even if they had the inclination, to sit by a whelping bitch, stop-watch in hand, checking how long it took each puppy to find the 'milk bar'. But any breeder who really enjoys rearing a litter will, by the time they are six weeks old, have a good idea of their individual characteristics. Unfortunately many breeders are unable to apply this knowledge in assessing how these individuals will grow up.

As I say, the boldest puppy usually turns out to be the boldest dog provided he has the same opportunities as his brothers and sisters. He will be more dominant, have more initiative and more intelligence. But we don't know how bold he will be. He may be a hard, wilful, pack-leader type of dog, and you may not be the sort of person who can cope with him.

Here you should take breeding into consideration. If a puppy is bred from stock which is known to be hard and wilful it is probably better to leave the dominant one (very often there is only one or possibly two in a litter), especially if it is a dog. If, on the other hand, the ancestors are known to be submissive and anxious to please, go for the bold pup every time. If in doubt you are always on a better bet with an over-bold puppy than with an over-sensitive one.

Whatever you do, avoid the backward puppy, the one that is always behind and gets pushed around by its brothers and sisters. It will almost certainly lack initiative and probably intelligence too. And avoid like the plague the shy puppy which rushes into its kennel at the sight of a stranger. Many bold puppies turn nervous later but I have never known a nervous puppy turn bold. Some people feel sorry for the backward, nervous puppy. Many who have chosen one with a view to training it have lived to regret their decision.

Many shepherds have a method of picking a pup which simply puts all that I have just said into practice. They wait until the pups are asleep and then call them. The one that reaches them first is the pick. Another belief held by some shepherds is that the mother's favourite is always the best pup. There now seems to be evidence that the dominant pup nearly always *is* the mother's favourite. She washes it first (possibly because it is always first there) and it always sleeps nearest to her head. There is also evidence to show that if a bitch pushes a puppy out there is something wrong with it. Unfortunately these puppies, which Nature intended to die, are often hand reared. That in itself may be all right, but when they are bred from, it is likely that they will pass on some hereditary weakness.

Hereditary gun-shyness can be detected at a very early age. But there is no need to go armed with a gun to look at puppies. We simply clap our hands suddenly when the puppies are playing around and, if any run away, we leave them there. Sometimes, I may say, to the great annoyance of the breeder. Naturally, puppies conditioned to noise will stand up to this test better than those which are not. The trouble is that there is no way of telling whether a puppy could be conditioned to it. In any case a lot of puppies will stand up to it without conditioning and I would always choose one of them.

You will note that I have made many references to the age of six weeks to acquire a puppy. That is the age at which many breeders are only too pleased to let the puppies go and it is the minimum legal age at which they can be sold. But many reputable breeders won't let their puppies go until eight weeks. I used to belong to this category myself but now realize that, provided the new owner is capable of looking after a puppy of this age, there are advantages in his having it then. Take a puppy from a litter at six weeks, let it live indoors with human company for a fortnight, then compare it with the rest of the litter. Physically it won't look very different but mentally it will be streets ahead of its brothers and sisters. And it would be a long time before they caught up, if ever they did.

So far I have dealt with the choice of a puppy, but many of the best dogs I have owned have come into my hands at varying ages right up to nine years. And I have acquired most of these because someone else could not cope. There are many advantages in starting with an adult dog, the most obvious being that you can see what it is, instead of trying to assess what it may become.

Pedigree does not matter so much, as you can judge the dog itself to a certain extent. But it can be a help. If, for instance, you want a dog for tracking and are offered one that has never had the opportunity to track, to me the deciding factor here would be whether the dog was bred from tracking stock.

The usual snag with an adult dog is that it has acquired some bad habits. Indeed it is usually *because* he has developed some bad habit that an adult dog is looking for a home. This may or may not create a big problem. It depends on what the habit is, how firmly it has become established and what efforts, if any, have been made to cure it. And it also depends on how good you are at training.

Many bad habits are the fault of the owner rather than the dog. For the Southern Television series *Training the Family Dog* I bred a litter of puppies specifically for the purpose. This I did by crossing an English Springer dog with a Bearded Collie bitch. The dog was from a show/working strain of very hard dogs. The bitch, Fly, was from a Scottish working strain and was really a Border Collie with a Beardie coat. She was a good sheepdog, had an excellent temperament and was harder than the average Border Collie. Her litter sister was a quite outstanding gundog.

One of the pups was dominant right from the start. In the end, however, after much observation, thought and discussion we chose one not quite so dominant, but still an extremely bold and friendly pup. This was because we were afraid the dominant pup might prove too hard to demonstrate how to choose and train a *family* dog. By then we had discarded the other pups and called these two Ben and Spot.

By the time he was nine weeks old we found a home for Spot who was by then a pretty rowdy customer. His new owner took him one afternoon and brought him back about eleven that night. He had 'bitten' his little girl and howled when left alone!!

It is always unwise to rear two puppies together, as they develop an attachment for each other rather than for their human master. So for his own and Ben's sake we were anxious to find a home for Spot. A dog in the village which spent its whole life roaming the countryside suffered a similar fate to many of its kind and one day failed to return home. The owners, having heard we had a puppy, came to see us with a big sob story. Their boy was heartbroken, they had learned their lesson and would *never* let another dog roam, etc., etc. So we let them have Spot. And being local we frequently saw him in the village. If there was a crowd of boys playing football, cricket or just being rowdy Spot was there, right in the middle of them. He was everybody's favourite, he enjoyed life to the full, but he never seemed to be at home and we could foresee trouble.

Sure enough when he was about nine months old his owner arrived with him at our gate. He had dug his way into a poultry run and killed three chickens. The farmer was waiting to shoot him if he returned and if we did not take him back he was going to have him put down right away. So poor Spot was back again.

Training the Family Dog was still being filmed and it struck me as an idea that I might use Spot to demonstrate how to cure a dog of chasing poultry. He arrived at night and when let out in the morning he went straight for Daisy, an old goose we had at the time. Quick as a flash my wife (whose reflexes, like mine, are conditioned to this sort of thing) threw a handful of gravel at him, simultaneously with a very severe ticking off. The effect was strengthened by the fact that, instead of fluttering all over the place as Spot had expected, Daisy simply stood her ground facing him. When we took him out later to see if he would chase hens he would not go near them!

By now he really was wild and my wife set about giving him some elementary training. Most dogs which have had complete freedom resent discipline for some time. And Spot was no exception. For about a fortnight it was more a daily battle than a daily training session. Then he gave in and was soon really enjoying his training. In quite a short time he was well above Novice Class standard often seen in the ring. And he would face thickest cover, seek back and hunt all day for a lost object, a quality Ben also inherited.

As I said, one can usually pick the boldest puppy but one cannot tell how hard or soft it will turn out to be. We found that our fears of Spot being too hard were unfounded. It was Ben who was rather softer than we really like. We would have liked to have kept Spot, but he and Ben had more than a bad influence on each other. And, of course, Ben was by now established in the TV series.

This time we tried to find a home for Spot where his talents would be appreciated and, through a mutual friend, met an obedience enthusiast in Southampton, Mr Bowen Jenkins. His Golden Retriever was getting on a bit and he was toying with the idea of having a young dog to replace him.

So he had Spot when he was just a year old and started off by doing quite well in competitions. We had advised him from the start that this dog would do well in Trials and he suddenly decided to have a go. After only one month's practice he competed in his and Spot's first Working Trial – and qualified CD Ex. From there he went on to qualify UD Ex., WD Ex., and TD Ex. So this ex-delinquent now leads a happy life and provides a great deal of pleasure for his owner who has become a very good friend of mine. At one stage Bowen had ambitions to teach Spot manwork but I persuaded him not to do so. Spot would enjoy it all right, a bit too much for a dog that is going to be kept as a family companion.

Although Ben became one of the best known and most successful film dogs we ever owned, he developed kidney trouble at about seven years of age and died after two years of indifferent health. Spot became a consistent performer in TD trials and would have made just as good a film dog as Ben. We attended his fifteenth birthday party on 1 April 1984. He was a bit more sedate than in his youth but he was hale and hearty and still enjoys the occasional tracking session. So we really did pick the wrong pup!

There are many other examples I could give of dogs transformed from liabilities into valuable assets. The most important things to try to assess are the dog's inherent capabilities and how bad are the bad habits.

Apart from pet dogs wanting new homes, the bigger breeders often have young dogs for sale. Frequently they keep two of the same age to see which turns out the better show prospect, and then they sell the other one. It will be less likely to have developed bad habits than the dog brought up in a home. But it will be quite uncivilized and dogs brought up like this take quite some time to settle in a new home. They miss the other dogs and have very often developed a close relationship with one particular kennelmate, which does not help. Often they are difficult to house train, depending on the

system of the particular kennel. We once bought a young
adult bitch from a well known breeder. When she let several of
the dogs out for us to see she was furious because some of
them messed on her beautiful lawn. They should have done it
in their kennels where it would have been more easily picked
up! Not surprisingly the little bitch we bought was not very
reliable about being clean indoors. In spite of all that, a good
dog reared in kennels may be a lot better as a training
proposition than a bad one reared in a home.

While you should always find out as much as you can about
a dog's background you can also judge quite a lot from the
dog itself. First of all study the dog's expression. He should
look bold and alert, full of the joys of life, with a twinkle in his
eye. Avoid the sullen, miserable-looking dog or one with a
mean shifty look.

If you are a stranger the dog may not like you to begin with.
Fair enough. You probably don't want him to welcome
strangers to your home. But once you have been introduced
and accepted by his owner he should come up to you. Many
people claim that their dog is suspicious of strangers when it
is, in fact, terrified of them. I would never buy a dog which
would not allow me to handle it if its owner said so.

For your purpose the over-friendly dog is always the best
bet, especially if a youngster up to about eighteen months.
Think very carefully before buying a six-month-old puppy
which already shows a strong guarding instinct.

When you go to see a dog allow yourself time to study him
carefully. Allow him to potter around his garden or, better
still, get his owner to take him for a walk and allow him to run
loose. You don't want a dog that clings to its owner (especially
if you have Trials in mind) but neither do you want one that
never responds. If it sees something strange it should either
bark at it or go to investigate but *never* run away.

Watch how he moves. I have a bit of a 'thing' about
movement in both dogs and horses and get a great deal of
pleasure just watching a good mover in action. But few people
realize how much temperament affects an animal's action.
The gay, jaunty 'Here I come and who's like me' type always
has a spring in its step which is completely missing from the

one with a lethargic temperament. Of course, you must consider how fit the dog is at the time.

We now live in an age when dogs have many physical defects which were unheard of in the last century. Probably because dogs with PRA, hip dysplasia and all the others were promptly destroyed before they had the opportunity to pass on the defect. Because of this it is usually worth the expense of having a prospective purchase examined for any physical defects by a veterinary surgeon. He or she should be able to spot any mental defects too but, taken as a whole, the veterinary profession's ignorance of canine mentality is quite lamentable. I am pleased to say that vets are now showing far more interest in canine mentality than they did in the past. Unfortunately most of it is purely theoretical and gleaned from animal behaviourists, canine psychologists and others who use scientific terms and big words which I, for one, have difficulty understanding. Dog owners who come to me for advice after they have consulted their vet do not appear to have understood any better. Still it is good to know that vets have at last realized that dogs have brains as well as bodies and there is no doubt that their knowledge is improving.

2

Principles of Training

Association of Ideas – Correction and Reward

THE first essential to success in training is to get rid of any ideas you may have about dogs being 'almost human'. Thank heaven they are not! The main difference lies in the fact that dogs do not reason as we do. There is some difference of opinion as to whether dogs work anything out in their minds at all. I believe they do but, whatever views one holds about this, all training must be based on the *assumption* that *dogs do not reason*:

ASSOCIATION OF IDEAS

Dogs, like all other animals, learn by association of ideas. This simply means that if the dog does something (accidentally or intentionally) and finds that it provides pleasure he will associate the action with the pleasure and tend to repeat it. Likewise, if he does something which results in an unpleasant experience he won't be so keen on doing it again. It is up to you to see that the things you want the dog to do provide him with pleasure and that the things you don't want him to do provide the opposite.

For the purpose of training we provide the displeasure or pleasure by what are known as correction and reward. We therefore train a dog by using correction and reward to build up the associations of ideas that we want. Which simply means that if the dog does wrong we correct him and if he does right we reward him. *And it must be done at the time*. There is no good in telling a dog that he was very naughty this morning and therefore must go to bed without any supper tonight. One must scold him when he *is* naughty – not afterwards.

You must also take great care not to create wrong associations, which is much easier than people expect. There is, for example, the owner who, when a dog goes off rabbiting, waits till it comes home and then gives it 'a jolly good hiding'. He believes that he is punishing it for running away – whereas in the dog's mind it is being punished for coming home, the worst possible association to create.

One should praise the dog for coming back (though, speaking personally, there is no time when I feel less like praising the brute). I have yet to hear of anyone who has ever cured a dog of rabbiting by punishing it after it has come home. I'm afraid, too, that this kind of owner often goes on nagging at the miserable dog long after the latter has forgotten the crime – if, in fact, there was one.

As a further aid to training we can and should make use of the submissive instinct to which I have referred in the previous chapter. It is now generally realized that even wild animals such as 'big cats' in circuses will accept a human master as their 'boss animal'. This is much easier to achieve with a dog than with any other animal. Although dogs are not almost human, we are in many ways almost canine, and it is easy to take on the role of leader – provided, that is, we have a dog that wants to be led. Most animals are governed by what is known as the pecking order, so called because it was first studied scientifically with domestic poultry. In a flock of twenty-six hens, A will be the leader who bosses everyone. B will boss everyone except A and so on until we come down to poor Z, who bosses no one and is bossed by everyone. It is not quite as simple as that with a pack of dogs but that is the principle.

Exactly the same thing takes place in many other social orders, including the human one. The result is that, while practically anyone can make a 'Z dog' obey, only those with A-plus will-power can succeed with an 'A dog'. This brings us back to what I said about getting a dog with a temperament to suit your own. Lack of compatibility is the cause of far more failures than is generally realized.

I am frequently asked for advice on disobedient family dogs. Many of these will obey 'Dad' but refuse to obey 'Mum'.

Occasionally, however, I meet one which obeys the wife but pays not the slightest attention to the husband. In the cases I have been able to observe closely I have invariably found that the husband obeys the wife too!

CORRECTION AND REWARD

Returning to correction and reward: what do they mean, and to what extent should they be applied? On this there cannot be hard-and-fast rules, but on a proper balance between the two the whole success of training depends – bearing in mind that to be successful one must not only get the dog to do what one wants, but to enjoy doing it. To some dogs a severe talking-to is all that is ever necessary by way of correction, but many others would treat life as one huge joke if corrected in that way. To some a friendly pat or a stroke on the head are sufficient reward, but others need fussing all the time to keep them 'alive'.

Methods of *Correction* vary according to the dog and to the exercise, but never hit a dog with a stick or other weapon, or raise your hand to slap him or, even worse, flap about with a folded newspaper as some people recommend. This is likely to make the dog (if he has any sense) keep out of range, and keep away from one's hand rather than come to it as one wants him to do. If he is a dominant dog with the slightest tendency to be aggressive he will accept this as a challenge and stand a very good chance of winning.

The first thing to do before correcting or punishing any dog is to get hold of him. The usual method of correction is to jerk a dog with the lead as and when he does, or attempts to do, the wrong thing. Chain slip collars hang quite slack and are more comfortable than buckled collars when not in use, but they can immediately be jerked up tight. They are almost universal in training circles but some dogs resent them and - will be happier in a leather collar. I deal more fully with collars on pages 48, 49 and 50. A good deal depends on the strength (mental and physical) of the dog compared with the strength of the owner. If no effect can be obtained by the simple chain slip collar, there are several quite effective training collars on the market which are decidedly uncomfortable when jerked up tight but quite comfortable, and therefore quite humane, when the lead is slack.

And if that fails, then I advise getting a smaller or more responsive dog! I always feel sorry for women in particular as they struggle and strain in trying to jerk some sense into a big, boisterous, powerful young dog – usually with no effect at all, except on themselves.

If a dog is deliberately disobedient and needs a severe reprimand I take a firm hold of him by the loose skin on each side of his neck, as in photograph 9, I look straight into his face, scold him and shake him – *really* shake him if necessary. This method of correction was taught to me by a shepherd long before I had ever heard of obedience training. It is still the most effective method I know to correct a wilfully disobedient dog. Great care should be taken, however, in using it on a young and/or sensitive dog, as it could completely demoralize it.

We now come to the equally, or even more, important subject of *Reward*. To me, it is a great pity that so many trainers appear to overlook its importance or are reluctant to use this aid to training. We see competitors, both novice and otherwise, stomping round an obedience ring with every muscle tensed, a look of grim determination on their faces, but never a word of praise for the dog which is probably doing its best to please.

How does one reward a dog? As I said, it depends entirely on the dog, and, to the ideal dog, a friendly pat and a kind word are all that are necessary. There are others, unfortunately, which couldn't care less whether one pats them or not. Some would much rather be left alone to enjoy their own pastimes. Some dogs respond to a lot of fussing, while others will, if fussed a lot, become far too excited and forget what one is trying to teach them. Generally speaking, patting or fussing the dog is all that is necessary by way of reward and the great majority of obedience trainers, I think, use and recommend that method.

The other method of reward is by food, and this is the method by which most pet dog owners attempt to train their dogs, and by which nearly all circus and stage dogs are trained. It is, however, a very controversial subject, and some trainers, for whose opinions I have the greatest respect, condemn its use under any circumstances. It should also be noted that the use of food is not allowed in competitions and it would be foolish to have a dog which always expected it.

My own experience is that some dogs will work much more quickly and show much greater enthusiasm if occasionally rewarded with food. Its use can be very valuable in some exercises, but worse than useless in others (I shall try to explain as I come to them). But the dog must be made to understand clearly that he must do what he is told, food or no food – it should be used only as an extra incentive to do it a bit better.

Such, then, is correction, and such is reward. We now come to the important and difficult matter of combining the two. If there are any 'secrets' in training, the ability to combine correction and reward properly is certainly one of them. It is a gift which many people try for years to acquire without success, while others appear to master it right from the start.

There are several rules to observe, the first and probably the most important being that you must correct or reward your dog according to whether he does wrong or right, not according to whether you yourself are feeling in a bad mood or a good one. That may seem obvious, but I am afraid that neglect of this rule is a far too common failing amongst those who try to train dogs. All of us, for many and varied reasons, feel a bit cross and irritable at times. That is not the mood in which to try to train a dog. My advice in those circumstances is to forget about training and simply take the dog for a romp. By doing so you will do no harm – the day off may do him and you a lot of good – but if you try to teach him something which he finds difficult you will almost certainly have a 'scene', which may prove a serious set-back. At this point, I might mention, too, that people who lose their tempers should never attempt to train a dog or any other animal.

The next important point is to correct or reward your dog as and when he does the wrong or the right thing. When he is in the process of learning some new exercise, make a point of praising and rewarding him *whenever he makes the slightest attempt to do what you want him to do*. This requires a great deal of concentration on the part of the trainer – but you cannot expect a dog to concentrate on you if you do not concentrate on him. Try to anticipate what he is going to do so that you can correct or reward him *as he does it* – not before or after.

Never correct a dog more than is necessary. This varies tremendously with different dogs. If he responds to a little jerk on a slip collar then just give him little jerks, but if he does not appear to feel a little jerk you must go on jerking harder and harder, *and harder*, until he *does* feel it. Never really punish a dog unless you are sure that he knows what he should do and is deliberately disobeying you. It is not always easy to be sure, but, if in doubt, give the dog the benefit.

Do not forget that dogs, like humans, can feel a bit off colour without actually being ill. If your dog does not appear to be enjoying the exercises which he usually likes, then make him do something quite simple which he likes doing, make a great fuss of him, and finish training for the day. He will probably be his usual self again tomorrow, but if you go on forcing him, you are likely to make him a sour and miserable worker.

By a co-ordination or balancing of correction and reward the dog should very quickly learn that it is much more pleasant to do what you want him to do, and he should try to please you. What is even more important is that, by doing so, he will learn to respect you and accept you as his leader. From that respect will develop a devotion far greater than can be developed by any amount of feeding, cuddling and slobbering over, regarded by many as essential if a dog is to become fond of them.

Right from the start build up a sense of respect in your dog by correcting him when he does wrong (as severely as necessary); by praising him when he does right; by never blaming him when you are to blame yourself; by never either over-rating or under-rating his intelligence. To put it briefly, be just and fair at all times.

So much, then, for correction and reward. We hope that

eventually, without any regard for either, our dog will do what we want, *when* we want. We must therefore find some means of conveying our wishes to the dog in the form of words of command and/or hand signals. A common mistake is to think that a dog knows the meaning of every word said to him. A dog does not understand words at all, in the sense that we know them. He understands certain sounds – probably a great number of different sounds – but they are only sounds, not words, to him. It does not matter whether you tell a dog to lie down by whistling to him or by saying Down, Flat, Lie, or even Sit or Stand. What does matter is that you always say the same thing, or rather make the same sound, for each exercise.

As his training advances, your dog is going to have to become acquainted with quite a large number of different commands, so make your commands as clear and short as possible. He will have to learn, for instance, that Down means down and Sit means sit, and it is a waste of breath and very muddling to the dog to say 'Sit down there, old boy', which is the sort of thing one so often hears.

Having decided what command you are going to use, the next thing is to make the dog associate each command with the particular exercise. To do so we go back to correction and reward. We give the command, for example Sit, correct the dog by forcing him (gently at first) into a sitting position, and when he is there (even if we have forced him into the position) praise him enthusiastically. By this method a dog of average intelligence very soon realizes the meaning of the word Sit and learns that if he sits promptly he will be praised, but if he does not, he will be corrected (quite severely when you are sure he knows what you mean). It is obvious, therefore, that by far the easiest and most pleasant course for the dog to take is to sit when he is told. Eventually, in the trained dog, no correction or reward is necessary.

To emphasize your words of command you must vary your tone of voice. This is a most important point in training and one which many have difficulty in mastering. A dog which knows and understands his owner can be scolded, praised, steadied or excited, all by the tone of voice – and by this I don't mean volume. It is possible to scold a dog very effectively in a whisper, as most experienced trainers who work dogs in public are well aware. Much of the bawling and shouting one hears in competitions is quite unnecessary, and in the eyes of the general public, a very bad advertisement for training. Dogs have much better hearing than humans, and a good shepherd can work a dog a mile or more away with a great deal less noise than some obedience handlers when the dog is about three metres away. People who get into the habit of shouting cannot raise their voices in an emergency. If one shouts in a scolding tone to a dog which is not usually shouted at, he will realize without any doubt that he is doing the wrong thing, and is likely to stop immediately.

Always use a harsh tone of voice in conjunction with your corrections, and a kind, encouraging tone with your rewards. The dog should then soon understand whether he is doing the right or wrong thing by the tone of voice alone. The harsh tone replaces the growl of the dominant member of the pack or of the dam when the puppies were in the nest. We are therefore strengthening our association of ideas by using the dog's natural instinct to react to this sort of noise.

Right from the start the dog should learn to associate a certain word (I use 'No') with doing the wrong thing. The degree of harshness should be varied according to whether he is being deliberately disobedient or simply does not yet understand what you want him to do. In the same way you can use a certain word or words, such as 'Good dog', in a kind tone every time you fuss or praise the dog when he does the right thing. In time it will be possible to praise him without touching him and when he is some distance from you.

And now we come to the commands or 'aids' which appeal to the dog's sense of sight, one of the few senses, if not the only one, in which some dogs are inferior to ourselves. You must not, however, underestimate his powers of sight, which can be a great help in training, and it is really quite amazing how slight is the movement of the hand or body to which a dog can be taught to respond. A good example of this is to be found in stage dogs, which are supposed to add, subtract, tell the time, and so on by barking a number of times. All they do in fact is to bark and stop barking on given signals which the audience does not notice – a movement of the head, putting the hand in a pocket, taking it out again, etc., etc. Experienced and clever handlers in obedience competitions sometimes adopt similar methods to get their dogs that little bit closer. Equally experienced judges usually spot it and take marks off for 'extra commands'!

There are certain movements to which the average dog will respond naturally, and the fullest possible use should be made of them in training. Perhaps the most important is the use of the hand. If your dog is fond of you and you hold out your hand he should come to it. This natural tendency is going to be of great value to you and you must *never* at any time do anything to kill your dog's trust in your hand.

If hand signals are used in conjunction with your words of command you will be making your commands doubly clear to the dog. If he is not quite sure of either (as he will not be to begin with) the two combined may make it easier for him. As his training advances, either the word of command or the signal can be dropped.

Most trainers drop the signals and keep the words of command. Others combine the two, using signals on the Distant Control exercise and words on the others. Some drop the words of command entirely and work their dogs, very successfully, solely by hand signals.

The use of hand signals in conjunction with words of command can be very useful in handling a working dog, and is practised by the great majority of gundog handlers and shepherds in everyday work. Sheepdog trial handlers, however, do not use them at all as, in order to respond to them, the dog must take his eyes off his sheep, a serious 'crime' in trials.

If you decide to use hand signals the important point to remember is to make them clear – and do not forget that a dog sees you from exactly the opposite angle from which you see him; he has to look up whilst you look down.

3

Initial Training

House Training – Preventing Bad Habits – Noisiness When Left
Alone – Starting on a Lead

HOUSE TRAINING

THE first thing many people do when they bring a puppy
home is to start house training it. And I am certain that efforts
in this direction completely ruin the temperaments of many
good dogs for life.

The first essential to any success in training any animal (by
success I mean an animal that works happily with you, rather
than for you) is to ensure that it likes you. It must therefore
associate your presence with pleasure.

But what do people do? They remove this young puppy, a
canine baby, from its mother, brothers and sisters, and they
take it into a strange and bewildering place. It is a known fact
that fear or nervous tension affects both bladder and bowels
(dogs are by no means unique in this respect) and when it is
put down a strange puppy will nearly always urinate. And
many owners will scold it or even punish it physically. But it
does not know what it has done wrong – indeed it may not
know what it has done – and it associates this punishment not
with the 'crime' but with the person, the place and everything
around it.

The effect is added to by the fact that the puppy is not old
enough to want a leader. All it wants is a protector – a mother
figure to give it confidence. Its own mother will by now have
corrected it for biting too hard in play and it will respond to
this type of correction. But she will not have corrected it for
relieving itself. Unlike her human counterpart she will know
instinctively that bladders and bowels must be emptied
frequently, especially when the animal is young.

But the human guardian does not stop there. He or she

39

goes out and leaves the puppy shut up indoors. On returning there is a puddle on the floor and the puppy is punished yet again. Not only is it punished for something it cannot help doing, it is punished *after the event*. If it has been left alone any normal puppy will rush to the door to greet its returning owner. Here is an opportunity to make a fuss of it so that it will associate the owner with pleasure. Instead it soon associates its owner with correction which it dislikes. Soon it won't go to the door but it will still leave puddles on the floor – because it has never been corrected for that and cannot help it anyhow.

This is the type of owner who says 'Of course he knows he has done wrong. He always looks guilty and hides in the corner.' Would you not hide in the corner if you knew that going to the door resulted in a beating up? Dogs rarely look guilty and then only exceptionally intelligent dogs which have a very close relationship with their master. But many dogs look frightened and it is quite natural for a young dog to adopt a submissive attitude in the presence of its superiors. The puppy to which I have referred is simply afraid of its owner. But if you take any submissive dog, stare at it and scold it in an angry voice it will 'look guilty' to the ignorant onlooker. In fact it would only be reacting in the same way as a wild dog does to the dominant member of the pack.

A great many shy, nervous and neurotic dogs are made that way by owners who fail completely to build up the correct associations of ideas. They accuse the dog of being stupid when in fact it is they who are stupid in failing to interpret their wishes to the dog. In the end the dog becomes stupid and a complete nervous wreck into the bargain.

House training rarely presents any problems to those who appreciate that young animals cannot go for long without relieving themselves and that puppies actually want to be clean. Like pigs, kittens and most other animals born in nests puppies will go away from the nest to relieve themselves as soon as they are old enough. (This is in contrast to chimpanzees and their close relatives human babies who have to wear nappies!) If this natural instinct is taken advantage of, all that is necessary is to encourage the puppy to go outside. Often it is only necessary to give it the opportunity.

Here the common mistake is the new owner's failure to concentrate on the puppy. Most puppies 'ask' to go out but not in a positive manner by barking, whining or going to the door as many adult dogs will do. But if you really concentrate you should soon be able to 'read' your puppy and, if you hope to train him, this is something you should be trying to do anyhow. It may just be a change in his expression or he may start looking in corners or going round in circles. Whatever he does you should be able to see that he feels uncomfortable. It is then that you should pick him up quietly and take him out. Don't just shove him out and shut the door or he will sit on the step and wait until you open it. He will then do what he intended doing where he intended doing it in the first place. Take him out and stay with him until he has relieved himself. Then praise him very well and bring him in. If you are reluctant to go out on a wet night remember that the puppy will have similar ideas and be even less likely to move from the step. Puppies nearly always want to relieve themselves when they wake up from a sleep and after feeding. Make a habit of taking the puppy out on both these occasions.

If you are unable to be with the puppy or to concentrate on it all the time – few people are – then a playpen is a great advantage. This should be placed on an easily cleaned floor and should have the puppy's bed in it. Newspaper can be spread on the floor of the pen and the puppy put in it if you go out or are too busy to keep an eye on him. This does not encourage puppies to be dirty indoors as one might expect. If he is out of his pen he will nearly always go towards it when he wants to go out. You can then take him out as already mentioned and because of this it is a good idea to have the playpen near the back door.

A playpen not only helps in house training. It also prevents the puppy getting into mischief (thus avoiding the necessity to correct it) and prevents him being trodden on, hurt or frightened in any of the many ways that can so easily happen in the home. It is in fact better to keep a puppy outdoors in a kennel with run rather than have it being a nuisance indoors.

Occasionally puppies lack the instinct to be clean in varying degrees. This is usually due to a puppy being brought up under dirty conditions where it had no opportunity to get away from the nest. Here correction will have to be applied. And you will have to be even more observant as this type of puppy rarely worries about finding a suitable spot – it just squats where it is. As it does so, pick it up quickly, tell him in a firm tone 'No' and take him out. That is *very* severe correction to the average young puppy and the important thing is to apply it *as the puppy does wrong*. If you do it properly once or twice the puppy will associate the correction with the 'crime' and when he feels uncomfortable will start to worry about it. He will then act in the same way as the naturally clean puppy and you should be able to 'read' him and proceed as before.

As I have already mentioned, if mild correction does not work, apply it more and more severely until it does work. And never forget to be equally lavish with your praise when the dog does what you want.

PREVENTING BAD HABITS

At one time I advocated not starting training until a puppy was nine to twelve months old, but a dog can learn a lot by the time he is nine months old. The owner of a six-month-old pup which chased cars and ripped the place to pieces once said to me: 'Of course I could not start training him until last week.' When I asked why she said: 'The instructor at the local training class said that puppies should not be trained until they are six months old.' What the instructor probably meant was that puppies should not be taken to training classes until they are six months old.

Yes, puppies do learn a lot and there is ever-increasing evidence to show that they learn at a much earlier age than was at one time imagined. While I am dead against disciplinary training for young puppies, I believe that not only should bad habits be prevented but natural tendencies to develop good habits should be encouraged as they appear – irrespective of age.

If your puppy wants to retrieve encourage him. If he sits when you prepare his dinner tell him to do so. If he barks with excitement encourage that too – but make very sure he stops when you tell him. These are just some of the things a puppy can be encouraged to do as early as six or eight weeks which will be beneficial to his more serious training later on. The important point to bear in mind is that the younger the puppy the more the training must be a game rather than a lesson. And I might add, women are, generally speaking, better than men at this type of training.

By far the easiest way of preventing bad habits is to avoid, as far as possible, circumstances which are likely to lead up to them. This method will produce far better results than trying to cure a very young puppy by scolding and bullying him.

Remember that every time you tell a puppy to do something and he disobeys (either deliberately or because he does not understand) you have gone back a step; whereas every time you tell him to do something and he obeys (either because he understands or because he happened to be doing that anyhow) you have gone forward a step – perhaps a very small one, but certainly in the right direction.

Do not, therefore, put yourself in a position where your puppy is almost certain to disobey you. Whether or not this disobedience is intentional makes little difference. If you allow it you will encourage a repetition.

If your puppy sits for half a minute and gets up when you tell him, that is a step forward. If he sits for half-an-hour and gets up of his own accord, that is a step back. Do not, therefore, give a command unless you are in a position to see that it is obeyed. It is no use saying, 'Oh! I don't have time now; I'll try again tomorrow.' If you have not time now then don't give the command, and remember that it is worse than useless to give commands which your puppy is quite incapable of understanding.

A dog should be educated by gradual building up of associations of ideas, starting with simple ones and going on to the more difficult. The first idea which the average puppy learns is to associate its name with food. You call your puppy by name and you give him his food. Soon he learns to associate the sound of his name with a reward. There is nothing extraordinary about this, and almost any animal, either wild or tame, will come for food in response to a certain sound. Whole flocks of poultry and herds of cows rush to the sound associated with food.

A whole litter of very young puppies will very quickly learn their own names if called by them and fed in separate dishes, and the vast majority of puppies kept either as house dogs or in kennels *do* know their names.

Why then, if it is easy to teach a dog his name, do so many refuse to come when called?

This is one of the commonest faults that the professional trainer has to deal with, and I am certain that nearly all dogs which develop this habit do so because they are *taught* by their owners not to come when called. No one, of course, does this intentionally, but by building up a wrong association of ideas, many owners actually teach their dogs to regard the sound of their names as a signal to keep well out of range. This can best be explained by taking as an example a mistake, often made by those who never punish their dogs at all, and who would never intentionally be unkind to them.

The owner of quite a young puppy takes it for a walk, starting off in a built-up area where, unless small enough to carry, the puppy must be kept on a lead. At this stage he probably hates the collar and lead, and also hates all the traffic. When a park or a quiet country lane is reached, the lead is taken off and the owner and puppy have a most enjoyable walk. After a time, and probably when the puppy is still enjoying himself scampering around, the owner decides that it is time to go home. He calls the puppy by name, whereupon it bounds straight up to him. Without receiving a word of praise, it is then put back on the lead and dragged through the traffic, possibly to be shut in a kennel when it gets home. As the puppy hates both the lead and traffic, this may be just as much of a punishment as severe correction. 'Once bitten, twice shy' applies to dogs just as much as to humans, especially to intelligent dogs.

What the owner is doing in this case is teaching his puppy to associate its name, not with a reward (as he did earlier by feeding) but with a punishment. So who can blame the puppy for saying to himself 'I know what happened last time', and refusing to come next time it is called. A bad habit is started which, like all bad habits, has a nasty way of getting worse.

How, then, do you set about encouraging your pup to come when his name is called? It is no use saying you should never put a puppy on a lead after calling him to you, for, of course, sometimes you have to. What you can do is to make a point of calling him many times when you are *not* going to put him on his lead. When you take him for a walk don't wait until you are ready to go home, but call his name when he happens to be coming to you. As he reaches you, make a great fuss of him or give him a tit-bit – and let him go. Do this several times during a walk so that your puppy will associate his name with a reward and, even if you sometimes do put him on a lead, he will not know whether you are going to do so or give him the tit-bit. You can also, as far as possible, follow up anything which the puppy dislikes with something pleasant: in other words, by rewarding him. If he dislikes crowds and traffic, as many young puppies do, take him out just before feeding time so that he returns to a nice meal which may help to compensate for his unpleasant experience.

These are just examples of the many ways in which you can help your puppy to understand his first word of command, his name. At this stage you must get him to understand that when he hears it he should come to you and that he will be rewarded for doing so. Later on, as he becomes more educated, he will learn to associate the word in different tones with different meanings, but at present it means that you want him to come to you and you must, therefore, always use it in an encouraging, pleasant tone. You may like to use a word of command such as 'Come' or 'Here'. If so, the dog's name should be used in the same friendly tone.

The best reward at this stage is, in my opinion, food. Small puppies, like small boys, usually appreciate it more than other forms of praise. But you can pat him, and make a fuss of him, and tell him that he is a good dog, in a praising tone of voice.

In short, do everything you can to get your puppy to come to you quickly, not because he *has* to, but because he *wants* to.

NOISINESS WHEN LEFT ALONE

Oddly enough, very few people, experienced trainers as well as novices, take any trouble to teach a puppy to remain quietly where he is left until his owner returns. This may seem a very trivial and unnecessary exercise. However, when one considers the number of dogs, including winners in obedience classes, which create pandemonium when left on the bench at a show, and the number of people who cannot go from home without their dogs in case of complaints from neighbours, one realizes how necessary it is.

The trouble usually starts the very first night a puppy goes to a new home. Everything is all right until the household retires to bed. Then the puppy realizes that he is all alone, away from his brothers and sisters in strange surroundings; so he begins to howl. Here the fatal mistake is usually made by some kind-hearted member of the family getting up to console the puppy. It does not take an intelligent puppy long to realize that all he has to do is make a noise and someone will arrive to cuddle him and perhaps give him tit-bits. To save the owner the trouble of getting up, the puppy may be allowed to sleep in the bedroom, and thereafter refuses to sleep anywhere else. This state of affairs usually goes from bad to worse. It is very nice to have a dog that is one's 'shadow', but there are occasions when the average civilized human being does not want a dog with him.

It is no use scolding the puppy at this stage, as he will not understand you and you will only make him more miserable and probably distrustful of you. I hope, too, that very few of my readers would be so unkind as to scold a puppy just because he is miserable. You can, however, leave him alone. Some people may consider that a bit unkind, too, but if you put a puppy in a box with a comfortable bed, he may howl for a bit, but the chances are that he will soon settle down and go to sleep. A hot water bottle will almost invariably encourage him to do so.

A mild sedative or tranquillizer obtained from your vet is a good stand-by. This can save a puppy (not to mention yourself and your neighbours) a worrying and sleepless night or two. It should, of course, be reduced and discontinued as quickly as possible.

Never go back to him when he is actually making a noise or you may give him the idea that he has only to make a noise to attract attention. Wait for a break (probably a short one) then go back and praise him *for being quiet*.

The other common example of the dog which cannot be left alone is the one which has been reared in kennels, always in the company of other dogs. If he goes to a new home, or is taken out on his own and left by his owner – as on the show bench – he will often create pandemonium.

This very bad habit can often be prevented by teaching the puppy, when quite young, to stay in all sorts of odd places, either shut up or tied up. Do not at this stage try to teach the 'Sit' or 'Down' but simply teach the puppy to *stay* and see that he has no option but to do so. Go out of the room, turn round as you leave, give a firm command 'Stay', and shut the door. If the puppy scratches at the door or starts to bark, rush back to him and scold him severely. If you have been training him on the right lines, he will now understand the meaning of 'No'. If not, this is a good opportunity to make him understand. Repeat this as often as necessary, scolding more severely each time, until he remains quiet. When he does, do not leave him too long, but go back and praise him before he starts barking again.

Soon he should associate a severe scolding with making a noise. He should also learn that you are only leaving him temporarily and that, if he remains quiet, you will return to praise him. This treatment can be adapted to a wide variety of conditions. Tie him to a peg whilst you do a bit of gardening; or shut him in your car; or leave him tied up in all the odd places you can think of.

If you follow this advice, your puppy should grow into a dog that you can leave anywhere without your feeling ashamed of him. If you always use the same command, by the time you come to teach the Long Down, your dog will know the command 'Stay'. You will then only have to teach him the Down, and are likely to have much less trouble than the average trainer when you come to the 'Down out of Sight'.

STARTING ON A LEAD

So far as actually walking on a lead is concerned it does not really matter at what age you start. A dog which has never had a lead on till a year old will go just as well as one started at six weeks.

But no dog should ever be taken on the road or street without a lead and you don't want to leave taking him out until your puppy is a year old. On the contrary you want to get him out and about as soon as possible. The only reason why he should not run on the street at six to eight weeks is the risk of infection before he is inoculated. There is, however very little risk if you carry him, unless you are unlucky enough to meet some dog lover who wants to 'love' him, but, unknown to you, has just left her puppy at home dying of hard pad. You can also take him in the car. There is no doubt at all that the sooner a puppy is taken out and about the less risk there is of car sickness, shyness of strangers or fear of noise. As they become older, puppies become more and more likely to be upset by strange experiences especially during teething from four and a half to five and a half months.

Before you take your puppy out into strange and possibly frightening surroundings he should be happy on a lead. Otherwise you are subjecting him to two unpleasant experiences (the lead and the traffic, etc.) at the same time. All training should start in a place familiar to the dog. Unless a puppy will trot around house and garden quite happily on a lead don't drag him out into the street.

There is much difference of opinion as to the best type of collar to start a puppy so we might consider the various types of collar with their advantages and disadvantages. (Photograph 1.)

1.THE ORDINARY BUCKLED LEATHER COLLAR is frowned on by some simply because it is old-fashioned. Nevertheless it has its

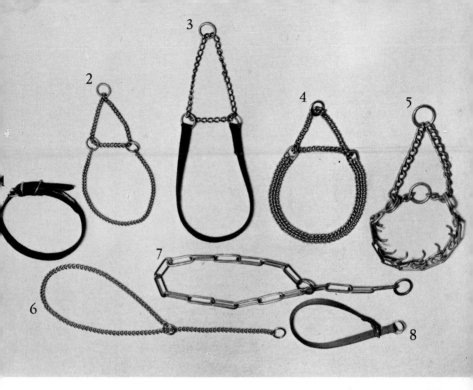

1. Various collars referred to in the text.
1) Buckled leather collar
2) Double action slip collar – single chain neckpiece
3) Double action slip collar – nylon web neckpiece
4) Double action slip collar – double chain neckpiece
5) Continental training collar
6) Single action slip collar – watch chain link
7) Single action slip collar – large link
8) Single action slip collar – nylon web.

2. Single action slip collar. Note lead in left hand when facing the dog to put the collar on.

3. Double action slip collar – lead slack.

4. Double action slip collar – lead tight. The neckpiece is tight enough to prevent the dog slipping the collar but long enough to avoid a choking effect.

5. Heel on lead. Note the dog's 'happy natural manner' with his
nose pointing forward in the direction he is going. Lead looped over
the thumb in right hand, hanging slack enough to reach dog's chest.
Left hand encouraging the dog to keep his shoulder 'reasonably
close to the left knee of the handler'.

6. Sit – first method. The dog was walking to heel on a lead when the handler halted, at the same time moving his hand over the dog's head. The dog should have his hindquarters closer to handler's left foot.

7. Sit – second method. Right hand pushing down on the rump, left hand pulling back on the lead.

advantages, the first of which is that it is adjustable. If you buy one for a puppy and it has to be taken up to the last hole it can then be let out as the puppy grows and will last quite a long time. Secondly it can be left on the dog with practically no risk of becoming caught up in anything and, of course, it can (by law it should) have your name and address on it. So far as the puppy is concerned he can run around wearing a collar until he completely ignores it before having a lead attached. Later on he can be left tied up on it if necessary.

The disadvantage is that, unless it is fairly tight, some puppies learn to slip a leather collar. But in most cases it is the owner who pulls the collar over the dog's head rather than the dog which slips its head out of the collar. If care is taken in the initial stages so that the puppy feels it cannot escape it is unlikely to keep trying.

2. THE CHAIN SLIP COLLAR is by far the most popular training collar and has been for many years. But we are not training the puppy yet, we only want to familiarize it with the collar and lead. For this purpose a chain slip collar is not ideal. No animal will choke itself on a noose unless it somehow gets caught up in something. But you are still at the stage where you are trying to make the puppy believe that you are a very nice person. And no one (not even the puppy) is likely to believe that if you give the impression that you are trying to strangle it!

Another disadvantage is that it is dangerous to have a puppy or even an adult dog running around wearing a slip collar, or, worse still, tied up on one.

The big advantage is that no dog can slip this type of collar and when it is slackened it hangs quite loose. It also has advantages in training which I shall be discussing later.

There are two types of chain slip. One with large links and one with flat watch-chain-type links. I much prefer the latter, though I know many excellent trainers who disagree.

3. THE DOUBLE-ACTION SLIP COLLAR is more modern than the ordinary slip and in my opinion an improvement on it in many ways. But it must fit properly and there is no

adjustment. It does, however, have some advantages if it fits properly. The dog does not feel that it may be strangled, but at the same time it cannot slip it (see photographs 3 and 4). It cannot be put on the wrong way round and the dog can be led on either the left or right. This may not appear much of an advantage to those with only competitions in mind. To those who want a more obedient dog it can be a very real advantage.

4. THE GERMAN TRAINING COLLAR is not really relevant to your present stage of puppy training but as we are discussing collars we might as well consider it here. This is rather a vicious looking affair which some animal welfare societies regard as cruel, but many of these do-gooders have a strong tendency to voice opinions on subjects about which they know nothing. In both Germany and France I have seen lots of dogs running around on their own wearing these collars. Dogs which show no sign of discomfort or distress and which look a lot happier and better cared for than many dogs I see in Britain.

It is many years since I first used one of these collars on a German Shepherd, Quiz, to whom I make several references later on. An ordinary slip collar had no effect on her whatsoever. I should really say that I was unable to have any effect on her by using an ordinary slip. Dogs are not trained by collars but by trainers who use collars properly. It is possible that I would have had Quiz put down had I not been able to get through to her initially by using a German collar. She felt it all right and that was my intention but I am sure she did not suffer nearly so much pain as many thin-skinned dogs do with a chain slip collar.

One might as well say that curb bits are cruel to horses. Many horses which wear them do suffer untold pain (horses suffer far more than dogs ever do) but it is not the bit which hurts; it is the person holding the reins who causes the suffering.

The German collar works on the same principle as the double action slip but the neck piece is made up of sections which have blunt spikes on the inside. Its size can easily be adjusted by adding or removing sections. I have used this collar on quite a number of difficult, insensitive dogs and found that it saved me a lot of hard work and the dog weeks of constant jerking with an ordinary collar. I only recommend its use on a dog that has proved to be unresponsive to a slip collar.

Which brings us to the question of finding one. Their sale is not banned in this country but because of our sentimental and impractical attitude to animals I do not know of anyone who stocks them. They can however, be purchased in any pet shop in Germany or France and I should imagine in most other European countries too.

Going back to the puppy I think the average owner will find that an ordinary leather collar is best (probably cheapest too). But if this does not prove successful try a double-action slip collar. As I said it must fit but it is quite easy to make one up with a piece of nylon cord or web and two rings.

It is a good idea to allow a puppy to become accustomed to wearing a collar before putting him on a lead. And never put a lead on a puppy until he will follow you without one. Once he does follow you, take him to a place where there is sufficient room, and where he is not likely to become mixed up with trees, clothes poles, etc. Put on the collar and a lead three or four feet long, strong enough to hold your particular pup but not any heavier than is necessary. A length of cord or light rope is better than a lead that is likely to break.

When they find they are held some puppies will fight it out there and then, doing everything possible to get away. All you have to do is stand still and hold on, turning round if necessary to avoid becoming a sort of human maypole. Very soon you can expect the puppy to stop struggling, probably quite suddenly. Some puppies hardly struggle at all and simply seem bewildered by the whole thing. Whatever the reaction of your puppy, you must praise him in a very reassuring manner, to impress on him that you do not want to do him any harm.

Call the puppy to you in a very coaxing manner offering food as a reward. If the puppy already comes to you without a lead as he should do there is every chance he will do so now. The lead should not be regarded as a means of making a dog

follow its trainer, only as a means of preventing it running
away. If you squat down and coax the puppy he should come
to you. If he does not, just wait. A puppy seems unable to
resist someone just sitting there. Anyhow, like any young
animal he won't stay still for long and, as the lead prevents his
going away from you, his only alternative to staying still is to
come to you. When he does, praise him well and proceed a
little further until he is trotting along nicely in response to
your coaxing (and tit-bits if necessary) not in response to the
lead.

You not only want your puppy to go on the lead, you want
him to enjoy going on it. Here the essential is to get him to
associate the lead with something he likes. As an example:
when you take him for a romp, *always* start on the lead,
whether you have to do so or not. Take him the first few
hundred yards on the lead, and then let him go. Very soon he
should regard the lead as a means to having a jolly good time,
and will be only too keen to go on it.

He may, in fact, become too keen, and start to pull. The
answer to that is not to pull *him*. Every time he pulls, *jerk* him
back, harder and harder, till he stops it, which he will do very
soon if you never let it become a habit.

As I shall be explaining in the following chapter, a dog
which pulls on the lead can usually be cured by a few heel
work lessons. It is always easier, however, to prevent bad
habits developing than to cure them once they have become
established.

4

Heel Work

Heel on Lead and Heel Free – Sit at Heel

WE have now come to the stage when your puppy is ready to start his obedience lessons proper, and I shall base my advice on how I should start a completely untrained young dog between ten and eighteen months old – a dog which is neither timid nor shy, and which is free from bad habits. If you have brought him up on the lines I have been recommending, you will find these exercises much easier, and, of course, if you have allowed him to develop any bad habits, you will find them much more difficult.

Before starting any lessons, the dog must know you, be friendly towards you, and be used to a collar and lead. At one time the first exercise I always taught was heel work. Experience, however, has forced me to change my mind on this. For the keen, headstrong young dog, especially if he has had no previous training, I still regard heel work as the best foundation on which to start. But the naturally obedient type that already follows to heel of its own accord can be (I believe often is) completely soured of all training by jerking about on the end of the lead. That heel work is not essential to obedience is proved by the hundreds of good working sheepdogs which have never had a collar on their necks. It is, however, essential in obedience competitions. Moreover, the sort of dog which is likely to do some good in competitions will either require some heel work lessons or will at least take to them willingly. We shall therefore start off with this exercise.

HEEL ON LEAD AND HEEL FREE

The explanatory notes for Obedience Classes are as follows:

1. Heel on lead

The dog should be sitting straight at the handler's side. On command the handler should walk briskly forward in a straight line with the dog at heel. The dog should be approximately level with and reasonably close to the handler's leg at all times, when the handler is walking. The lead must be slack at all times. On the command 'left turn' or 'right turn' the handler should turn smartly at a right angle in the appropriate direction and the dog should keep its position at the handler's side. Unless otherwise directed, at the command 'about turn' the handler should turn about smartly on the spot through an angle of 180 degrees to the right and walk in the opposite direction, the dog maintaining its position at the handler's side. On the command 'halt' the handler should halt immediately and the dog should sit straight at the handler's side. Throughout this test the handler may not touch the dog or make use of the lead without penalty.

2. Heel free

This test should be carried out in a similar manner as for Heel on lead except that the dog must be off the lead throughout the test.

In addition to the above, the Obedience Regulations for Class C Heel work state that:

The dog shall be required to walk at heel free, and shall also be tested at fast and slow pace. At some time during this test, at the discretion of the Judge, the dog shall be required, whilst walking to heel at normal pace, to be left at the Stand, Sit and Down in any order (the order to be the same for each dog) as and when directed by the Judge. The handler shall continue forward alone, without hesitation, and continue as directed by the Judge until he reaches his dog when both shall continue forward together until halted. Heel work may include left about turns and figure of eight at normal and/or slow pace.

In the Working Trial Regulations we are given the following information:

The Judge should test the ability of the dog to keep his shoulder reasonably close to the left knee of the handler who should walk smartly in his natural manner at normal, fast and slow paces through turns and among and around persons and obstacles. The halt, with the dog sitting to heel and a figure of eight may be included at any stage.

Any act, signal or command or jerking of the leash which in the opinion of the Judge has given the dog unfair assistance shall be penalized.

On top of that, the Kennel Club Explanatory Notes for Obedience Classes start by saying that 'In all classes the dog should work in a happy, natural manner and prime consideration should be given to judging the dog and handler as a team.' When this was emphasized in both Obedience and Trials Regulations one hoped that there was still a chance of dogs and handlers behaving naturally in the ring – and winning – a sight which had become more and more rare. When I competed in obedience most judges penalized heavily the dog which turned its head round the handler's knee. Today this seems to be the general practice and one sees top winning dogs with their heads screwed round to the right, staring up into their handler's eyes like half-witted idiots. This is not only unnatural – to the working-dog man and to the general public it is absolutely ridiculous. Who ever saw a shepherd, a gamekeeper, or a policeman on the beat with a dog behaving like that? A dog which lags slightly behind is of much more practical value and certainly less of a nuisance than one which keeps pushing against one's left knee.

In spite of its being so clearly stated in the rules it would appear that there are few judges around who recognize natural behaviour when they see it; judges who will not penalize a dog for being '*approximately* level with and *reasonably* close to the handler's leg' – and who will give 'prime consideration' to the dog working in a 'happy natural manner'.

Everyone knows the advantage of a dog that walks properly to heel – or at least the disadvantages of one that does not. What is not so often realized is that this exercise, being the first, is that in which one gets the dog's mind to co-ordinate with the trainer's actions and tone of voice. Once that is done, the other exercises become much easier.

As with all exercises, start in a place familiar to the dog where there are unlikely to be any distractions. If you are using a chain slip collar use one of the watch-chain type, and be sure you put it on the right way. To do so, face the dog as in photograph 2 and, with the ring to which the lead is attached held in the left hand, slip the chain noose over the dog's head. This means that the ring through which the chain slips comes under the dog's neck. When the dog is on your left side you can then jerk the chain up quickly. Just as important, it will instantly fall slack when you slacken the lead. If you put it on the wrong way round the ring will come over the dog's neck and tend to stay there when you slacken the lead. The next essential is a strong, pliable lead at least three feet long. Attach this to the collar which should fit comfortably with the ring under the dog's neck. Now stand facing in the same direction as the dog, with him on your left side. Hold the lead in your right hand with your elbow bent at a right angle. Allow the lead to be long enough for the loop, where it bends, to hang about halfway between the dog's neck and the ground. Always keep in mind that the right hand is the correcting hand and the left hand the rewarding one.

Now move off quickly, saying the dog's name, followed by a sharp 'heel'. It is unlikely that the dog will move as quickly, and you will automatically jerk him with the right hand. This should bring him up to you, when you must *immediately* reward him by caressing and fussing with the left hand. This is easy with a big dog whose head is just about level with your left hand, as in photograph 5, but not nearly so easy with a little one.

If the dog is a 'puller' and rushes forward on the lead, let him go and, at the exact instant when he is about to reach the end, turn sharp right, give a sharp 'Heel', and at the same time jerk with the right hand so that you have his own strength combined with yours in the jerk. Keep on turning right, both at right angles and right about, jerking him round, but never forgetting to praise and encourage with the left hand. Pat your thigh, caress his cheek with your fingers, or in fact do anything that you find will get him closer to you. In obstinate cases you can occasionally turn left and 'crash' into the dog, but too much of this will tend to keep him away from you rather than bring him closer.

Make all your movements quick and 'alive'. Keep turning in different directions so that the dog does not know which way you will turn next. Never work to a set plan, and remember that, as well as getting the dog to keep close to you, you are trying to make him concentrate on your actions. This he should do when he realizes that every time his mind wanders he receives a sharp jerk, but that he will be praised and fussed when he pays attention. If you are unfortunate enough to have a dog that lags, you will have to do much more rewarding than correcting, and give very short spells of training.

The degree of jerking, of course, varies considerably from dog to dog. If I were to give a terrific jerk on a chain slip collar to a thin-skinned, sensitive dog like a Greyhound, it would amount to downright cruelty and the dog would probably crumple up and go to pieces on me. On the other hand, if I gave a little jerk, to which a Greyhound would respond, to a powerful young German Shepherd, which had been pulling its owner all over the place since it was three months old, it would not feel it at all. With a big strong dog a good deal of physical strength is necessary in the initial stages, and that is one reason why many owners, particularly ladies, put in a tremendous amount of hard work with absolutely no result.

In this exercise I have found that rewarding with food does no permanent good, and may even do harm. It will get a dog to keep up with you so long as you have food in your hand, but that is not allowed in competitions, and one cannot go around constantly offering pieces of meat. It also encourages a dog to walk slightly ahead of the handler looking upwards and backwards for its reward. And that can end up as the abominable habit to which I have already referred.

You may now have your dog doing heel work very nicely on the lead, he is keeping right up alongside your left leg to receive that little encouragement from your left hand, and turning sharply to the right when you turn, in order to avoid that sharp jerk on the lead. If he does these things – but not unless – then you can try a bit of 'Heel free'. Here you are likely to find out whether or not you have been training in the right way. If you have, and if you have the right dog, he will do his heel work just the same off the lead as on. If, on the other hand, you have been jerking at him in a mechanical and lifeless sort of way, without rewarding him *at the right time*, he will in all probability follow you in some sort of way, either well behind or away to your left. In this case slip on the lead and start again, trying to get him to respond to the left hand,

and using the right one only when that fails. Remember that when you take the lead off you still have your left hand for encouragement, but your right (correcting) hand is gone.

Quite a number of the 'naughty' type of dog, when the lead is removed, make a dash for freedom even if they have been doing heel on lead quite well. Fortunately they almost invariably rush ahead, and the best and quickest way I have found to stop their rush is as follows:

Halt as usual with the dog sitting to heel on the lead; remove the lead and hold both ends in the right hand so that the lead hangs in a loop by your side, where the dog cannot see it. Now start off smartly in exactly the same way and with the same commands as you have been using. Try to keep him to your left side by encouragement with the hand but, if he is the sort of dog I have in mind, he will walk a few steps and then, with hardly any warning, go off like a shot from a gun. As he does so, not before or after, give him a 'stinger' on the hindquarters with the lead. He should, and almost invariably will, stop dead and rush back to you for protection, whereupon you must praise him very well indeed. No dog, even the very boldest, likes to be hit by something out of the blue.

Although this method sounds very easy it has its snags. First of all, you have only a split second in which to act, and it will test your powers of concentration and ability to anticipate what the dog is going to do. Secondly, it will test your ability to praise your dog instantly when he does the right thing. If you do it properly, it is unlikely that you will ever have to do it again. If you miss him and he does not notice that you tried to hit him, you will have done neither good nor harm, and can try again. I must warn you, however, that if he sees you make a wild swipe at him and you miss, you will be a lot further back than before you started. It is up to you, and do not forget to give a sharp 'Heel' as you go to hit him, so that the next time you say 'Heel' as he decides to go, he will associate it with that sudden smack which 'descended upon him from Heaven'. Instead of running away he should come closer to you.

Don't keep on saying, 'heel, heel, heel'. Don't ever give a command unless you are in a position to see that it is obeyed. This is straightforward association of ideas. The object is to make the dog associate 'heel' with correction (a jerk), in anticipation of which he will respond to the sound. You add to this by getting him to associate coming close to you with reward, in anticipation of which he should want to come of his own accord. Whether he responds more to the correction or reward depends chiefly on the dog. Most dogs respond in some degree to both, but remember that, provided he has done something to deserve it, you cannot over-reward a dog. A sensitive dog can, however, be completely upset by over-correction.

SIT AT HEEL

On the command 'Halt' the handler should halt immediately and the dog should sit straight at the handler's side.

Although the exercises are called 'Heel on lead' and 'Heel free', it is probably true to say that as many points are lost by dogs not sitting properly as by dogs not walking properly to heel. Actually it is a very practical exercise. It is much easier to teach a dog to sit still than to stand still. In a crowd it is just as important that a dog should stay close to you when you are standing as when you are moving, and he will occupy less space sitting than standing or lying down.

As soon as the dog is walking on a loose lead and coming up close to you in response to your left (rewarding) hand you can start teaching him to sit automatically every time you halt. There are several ways to make a dog sit (it is not usually very difficult) but I use either of two.

For the first, start with heel on lead until the dog is moving smartly in the right position close to your left leg. Stop suddenly and at the same time give the command 'Sit', swing your body round to the left (do not move your feet), and move the right hand over his head as in photograph 6. About fifty per cent of dogs will look up to the trainer's right hand and, when the movements are combined with a sudden halt, will go down on their haunches. The whole thing must be carried out simultaneously from a walk. There is no good stopping and then moving your right hand in the hope that the dog will sit. It must be done *as you halt*.

You may, however, have the other kind of dog, which will just stand and look at you as though you had gone a bit odd. In this case you will have to force him into a sitting position by pulling back on the collar with one hand, and at the same time pressing on his rump with the other as in photograph 7. See that he sits either square on his haunches or on the side which brings him towards you. If he is obstinate, you can grip the loose skin or hair on his rump with the hand pressing him down.

The first method is much less laborious than the second, and, being a firm believer in doing everything the easiest way, I always try it first, and if it fails, go on to the second.

Whichever method you adopt, be sure to praise your dog very well whenever he sits, and try to get him close up to you right from the start. If he sits wide of you, do not move towards him. Move to the right, *away* from him, and coax him up with your left hand. If necessary, swing his haunches towards you with the same hand as he sits down.

Never move towards your dog, except when returning to him after a Sit or Down. *Always* make him move towards you.

Do not keep on gently pushing him into a sitting position every time you halt. That will teach him nothing, and will only get him accustomed to being pushed down. Be gentle to start with but, if he does not respond, gradually replace the push with a slap on the rump. Remember that a dog must not only do what you want, *he must do it quickly*. A dog that is a bit slow and stubborn on his Sits can often be speeded up by combining the two methods already described. Stop suddenly, swing the right hand right over the dog and, with the tip of the lead which is held in that hand, give him a sharp smack on the rump.

Never forget to praise him when he sits – especially the first time he shows the least inclination to sit of his own accord.

In all heel work, make your movements quick and 'alive'. Also it is a good idea to repeat each exercise several times until the dog grasps it. For instance, halt, say 'Sit', push the dog into a sitting position; praise him. Then, halt, say 'Sit' and, as you go to push him down, he goes down himself; praise very well.

Finally, halt, say 'Sit' firmly and he does so of his own accord; praise very well indeed and go on to another exercise or finish for the day.

It is unlikely that he will do it as soon as the third time, but that is the idea, which can also be applied to the right turns and about turns. Repeat each exercise until you get some sign of response; praise very well, and leave it for the day. Next day you will be able to start where you left off, and so will steadily progress. If you keep on and on, the dog will sooner or later become bored and you will be further back than when you started.

And don't forget that trainers can become bored too. No use expecting enthusiasm from your dog if you are fed up with the whole proceeding.

5

Sit and Stay

FOR Obedience Classes we are told:

Sit/Stay

The Judge or Steward will direct handlers to positions in the ring. The command 'last command' will be given and handlers should then instantly give their final command to the dogs. Any further commands or signals to the dogs after this 'last command' will be penalized. Handlers will then be instructed to leave their dogs and walk to positions indicated until ordered to return to them. Dogs should remain at the Sit position throughout the test. This is a group test and all dogs must compete together, but where this is impracticable at an indoor show the class may be equally divided but the judging for the groups must be consecutive.

The Working Trials Schedule says:

Dogs may be tested individually or in a group or groups. The Judge or Steward will give the command 'last command' and handlers should then instantly give their final commands to the dogs. Any further commands or signals to the dogs will be penalized. Handlers will then be instructed to leave their dogs and proceed to positions indicated by the Judge or Steward until ordered to return to them. Where possible, such positions should be out of sight of the dogs but bearing in mind the short duration of the exercise this may not be practical. Dogs must remain in the Sit position throughout the test until the Judge or Steward indicates that the test has finished. Minor movements must be penalized. The Judge may use his discretion should interference by another dog cause the dog to move.

I should say that only a minority of trainers succeed in getting anything like a hundred per cent results in the Sit and Stay exercise. Considering the way some people start teaching it, I am not surprised. They make the dog sit, stand facing him, and then they move back a couple of steps to the end of the lead. If the dog remains sitting, he is then called up and praised well. By this method the trainer does not praise the dog for obeying his command to sit. Instead he praises it for getting up – the very thing he does not want it to do. Added to this is the fact that the chief reason for a dog's not remaining on the Sit at this stage is that it wants to be with its master.

It surprises me that any dogs taught by this method do remain sitting at all, and I am certain that it produces the vast numbers of dogs which are thoroughly unreliable on this exercise.

Before starting the exercise, do a bit of heel work to get your dog settled down. Now halt with your dog sitting to heel. With the lead still in the right hand move very slowly round to face him, saying very firmly, but not in a scolding tone: 'Sit – Stay'. Now move slowly back a couple of steps and pause. If he remains sitting go back to him immdiately, before he has had time to get up, and praise him well *for having stayed there*. Repeat this once or twice, gradually increasing the time you leave him sitting. Now move a bit to the right and a bit to the left, and gradually get him to allow you to move right round him – which he probably will not like to begin with.

This is the stage at which I usually finish the first lesson, and it is important not to make any hasty or jerky movements. If he moves to get up, take hold of him quickly by the collar (before he has time to get to his feet) and with your hand under his chin, pull his head up towards you, and then force him back on his haunches, at the same time saying 'Sit' in a very angry tone. Don't forget to praise him when he does.

For the next stage, start as before, but when you go back to praise him, slip the lead very surreptitiously onto the ground, then move back again, this time without the lead. Keep moving backwards away from him, a little farther each time, and always return to praise him for sitting. Concentrate on your dog, and try to get him to concentrate on you by raising your hand and by moving it to attract his attention if he looks away.

When you are able to walk back some distance, try turning

your back, but take a glimpse over your shoulder, as many dogs will get up the first time you turn your back. If your dog *does* get up, go back as quickly as possible and make him sit quickly on *exactly the spot where you left him.*

If he goes down on the Sit, go back to him, and, holding your hand above his head, tap him gently on the toes with your toe. You may have to put the lead on, and hold it in the hand above his head. But don't just lug him up into a sitting position or stamp on his toes with your big foot. Encourage him, with the aid of the lead and tapping on his toes, to sit up of his own accord.

Always be careful not to rush back to your dog in a way that will frighten him. Go back as quickly as possible, but do it quietly, or he may get up and run away when he sees you coming.

You will have noticed (at least I hope you have noticed) that I have not, up to this stage, called the dog to me at all. The most important rule of all for success in this exercise is *never to recall a dog* until he is quite steady on his Sits and Downs.

In Beginners and Novice 'handlers may face their dogs' but only 'at the discretion of the judge'. In Test A we are not told what should happen but most judges make the handlers stand with their backs to their dogs. In Tests B and C and in Working Trials handlers have to go out of sight while dogs are left sitting in the ring.

If you gradually teach your dog to remain sitting while you move round him and away in all directions you should have little trouble in getting him to stay while you stand with your back to him. Remember that if the judge does ask you to stand with your back to your dog he will penalize you if he sees you squinting over your shoulder. And quite rightly too. Earlier on I explained about the dog's exceptional perceptivity. To some dogs a slight movement of the head is as effective as a firm command to 'Sit'.

Many points are lost in competitions because people, when training, often use commands or signals, sometimes quite unconsciously, which in competition are 'extra commands or signals'. When he goes into the ring the handler then either loses marks for using these commands or signals, or the dog loses marks because he is 'put out' by the handler not using them. In the early stages of training always use commands *and* signals to make it as easy as possible for the dog to understand. But *before* you enter for a competition make up your mind what you are going to use and accustom the dog to responding with confidence to the command *or* signal. Also accustom yourself to using it in a way that will not be penalized in the ring.

Do not try to teach a dog to stay while you are out of sight until he is quite steady when you are in sight. And here again the 'secret' of success is to do it gradually. Start off by moving quietly but quickly round a corner, behind a tree or whatever else happens to be handy, and coming back again immediately. Many dogs get up the instant the handler goes out of sight for the first time, but they get such a surprise if he returns and scolds them that they are less likely to do it next time. From there, go on gradually increasing the length of time, while never forgetting to praise the dog on your return. Generally speaking, it is easier to teach a dog to stay on the Down than on the Sit. Therefore, I do not usually teach him to sit while I am out of sight until I have taught him to stay down out of sight.

6

Down

The explanatory notes for Obedience Classes where it is called the 'Down/Stay' say simply that:

This test should be carried out exactly as for the Sit/Stay except that dogs will be left in the Down position throughout the test. This is a group test and all dogs must compete together, but where this is impracticable at an indoor show the class may be equally divided but the judging for the groups must be consecutive.

In Working Trials the Down exercise is the same for all stakes – ten minutes, handler out of sight. The Notes for Guidance are more explicit:

Down (10 minutes)

Handlers must be out of sight of the dogs who may be tested individually or in a group or groups. The Judge or Steward will give the command 'last command' and handlers should then instantly give their final commands to their dogs. Any further commands or signals to the dogs will be penalized. Handlers will then be instructed to leave their dogs and proceed to positions indicated by the Judge or Steward until ordered to return to them. Dogs must remain in the 'Down' position throughout the test until the Judge or Steward indicates that the test has finished. No dog will be awarded any marks that sits, stands or crawls more than its approximate body length in any direction. Minor movements must be penalized. The Judge may use his discretion should interference by another dog cause a dog to move. The Judge may test the dogs by using distractions but may not call it by name.

Whether you are training your dog for your own pleasure and satisfaction or for competition work, one of the most important of all exercises is undoubtedly the Down. It is worth noting that this is the one and only exercise which is taught to the average sheepdog before it is allowed to work sheep.

In Obedience Classes and Working Trial schedules, more points are awarded for this exercise than for almost any other, and the chances of being placed with a dog that is not steady on the Down are very slender indeed. It seems surprising, therefore, that there are so many failures, and I should say that during the course of a year more points must be lost on this exercise than in all others put together. This is due partly to temperament in the dog, but I think just as much to the tendency of so many trainers to try to run before they can walk.

No great skill is required in teaching a dog to lie down. It is simply a matter of forcing him to the ground – *and making sure that he stays there*. This can be done in several ways but the easiest I have found with a stubborn dog is demonstrated in photograph 8. With the lead running under the instep of the left foot pull up with the right hand at the same time pushing the dog down with the left one. Once you have him down keep your left foot close enough to his collar to prevent him getting up. With a more responsive dog you can grip the collar under the chin with the right hand and jerk the dog down as you give the command. If necessary push down simultaneously with the left hand on the shoulders.

The important point is to get him to associate this lying down with the command 'Down', 'Flat', or whatever you use, or with a hand signal. *As you push him down* give the command in a harsh tone. The majority of dogs, if spoken to harshly, will naturally creep or lie right down. Full use should always be made of any natural tendency such as this. Do not worry about him being cowed. He will soon get over that once he knows exactly what you want him to do.

The other important point is to praise him whenever he stays down. Some trainers disagree, maintaining that to praise a dog in this exercise will make him get up. That is quite true in the initial stages, but it can be overcome by balancing the correction and reward. You should then have a happy dog which stays down to please you, instead of a miserable one which stays down because he is afraid to get up.

So long as he struggles keep telling him harshly to 'Down' and force him to do so – gently if he is a sensitive dog. But, if he decides to be rough with you, you will have to be rough with him. Immediately he relaxes for a second, however, change your tone of voice and tactics completely and praise him well, yet quietly. If you excite him too much he probably will get up.

Do not give him the chance to start struggling again. Let him get up and start once more at the beginning. Very soon (the time varies considerably from dog to dog) he should go down on command, perhaps assisted by a slight push, and should stay down beside you.

From there, proceed exactly as with the Sit, until you can walk all round him, step over him, run away, run past him, jump over him and make all sorts of peculiar noises. What you must try to do is to make the dog understand *gradually* that, no matter what happens, he must not get up until you tell him to do so. If he should get up, go back to him quickly and quietly, without frightening him, but at the same time letting him know that you are very, very angry, and put him down firmly in *exactly* the spot he was on. This is very important, and it is worth making a mental note of a stone, twig or tuft of grass beside the place where he is lying. Do not put something down beside him or he may learn to stay beside an object belonging to you, and may not stay without it.

Teach the dog to stay down while you go out of sight in the same way as you have taught him to stay sitting. It is a good idea to have some sort of 'hide' from which you can see the dog without him seeing you. If, for instance, you watch him through a hole in a fence you can scold him as and when he moves. If he is the sort that thought you couldn't see him this will give him quite a surprise.

Don't teach him to go down from the Sit or give a lesson on the Down immediately after one on the Sit. Either of these practices tends to make a dog go down on the Sit, a very difficult fault to eradicate. Any similar exercises, likely to be confusing to the dog, should be taught entirely separately. For example, give a lesson on the Down, then some heel work, then the Sit. Or give a lesson on the Down in the morning and the Sit in the afternoon.

Far too many people train their dogs with one object in view – winning in competitions. They swot up all the exercises in the particular test and go through them in the same order day after day until the dog does them automatically in the same way as a performing dog goes through a routine. A clever dog very soon learns which exercise follows which, and will, if allowed, carry on without any command at all. That is one reason for so many dogs going down on the Sit. All they are doing is what they have been taught to do by constant repetition. That they do it a bit ahead of schedule shows intelligence and common sense. Which brings me to the reason why many dogs fail in the Down – the tendency to teach the Sits and Downs for competitions with one eye on the dog and the other on a watch. If people would forget about competitions and teach their dogs *obedience* they would get on a lot better. In particular, if they would teach them to go down and *stay down* at any time, in any place and under all sorts of distractions, they would find that they would stay in the ring. Instead, as soon as the dog will stay five minutes out of sight at home or at classes, they enter him in Class A, apparently overlooking the fact that in competitions one cannot correct a dog and put him back on the spot in the way I have already described. If the dog, in his first competition, stays four minutes and fifty-nine seconds, then gets up and goes out of the ring, he may have started a habit which could ruin all his future chances of winning. Next time he will perhaps stay four minutes then three, until eventually he gets up and follows his handler out of the ring – simply because he has not been and cannot be corrected for it.

It is foolish to enter a dog in Class A until he will stay down at least fifteen minutes out of sight at home and in as many strange places as you can possibly find. Any well-trained working dog will stay in the same place for an hour without getting up. Theoretically, a dog, having been told to 'Down', should stay there until he is told to get up, whether that be in half a minute, half an hour, or at the end of next week.

Always remember that if you have just started a lesson by

ordering your dog to 'Down' and the telephone rings, do not leave him and forget about him. He *should* stay there until you return, but he *may* not, so don't take the risk. Slip the lead on again and take him with you, making him lie down beside you where you can keep an eye on him. In any case, it is always a good idea for the dog to be thoroughly accustomed to lying beside you for quite long periods before you ask him to stay while you move away. This need not take the form of a set exercise. If, when you are having a meal, reading a book or watching television, you put a lead on the dog, make him lie down close to you with your foot on the lead, he will have no option but to stay there. From half an hour to an hour of this at irregular intervals and in a variety of places will do far more to steady a restless, fidgety dog than taking him to classes once a week.

7

Recall and Finish

RECALL

HERE we find the same exercise given different headings in Obedience Classes and Working Trials.

For Obedience we have:

PRE-BEGINNERS AND BEGINNERS

Recall from Sit or Down position at handler's choice. Dog to be recalled by handler when stationary and facing the dog. Dog to return smartly to handler, sit in front, go to heel – all on command of Judge or Steward to handler. Distance at discretion of Judge. Test commences when handler leaves dog.

NOVICE

Recall from Sit or Down position at handler's choice. Dog to be recalled by handler when stationary and facing the dog. Dog to return smartly to handler, sit in front, go to heel – all on command of Judge or Steward to handler. Distance at discretion of Judge. Test commences when handler leaves dog.

CLASS A

Recall from Sit or Down position at handler's choice. Dog to be recalled to heel by handler, on command of Judge or Steward, whilst handler is walking away from dog, both to continue forward until halted. The recall and halt points to be the same for each dog and handler. Test commences following handler's last command to dog.

In Classes B and C this exercise is incorporated in the send away, drop and recall:

After the dog has been dropped, handler will call the dog to heel whilst walking where directed by Judge and both will continue forward. No obstacle to be placed in path of dog. Simultaneous command and signal is permitted but as soon as the dog leaves the handler the arm must be dropped. (NB an extra command may also be a simultaneous command and signal, but an extra command must be penalized.)

71

In Working Trials we have:

Recall to Handler

The dog should be recalled from the Down or Sit position. The handler being a reasonable distance from the dog at the discretion of the Judge. The dog should return at a smart pace and sit in front of the handler, afterwards going smartly to heel on command or signal. Handlers to await command of the Judge or Steward.

I have already dealt at some length in Chapter 3 with how to get a young puppy to come when called. The same principles apply to an older dog when you are teaching him the 'Recall'. They may not work with a dog which has developed the habit of running away when called, but they should do if you have brought up your pup on the lines suggested.

Presuming that your dog is quite steady on his Sits and Downs while you are in sight, sit him in the usual way, walk away from him and turn to face him. Now call his name pleasantly, and he should come to you. Most people call the name, followed by a command – 'Come', 'Here', etc. It should be used in a praising tone of voice, combined, in the early stages, with moving your hands in front of and patting your thighs as an encouragement. You do not simply want your dog to come to you. You want him to come at the gallop and sit smartly in front of you. To achieve this concentrate on getting the dog to come to you (even if he knocks you down in the process) before worrying too much about the sit and finish.

The easiest way I know to persuade a dog to come to me at the double is to offer him food. This is the only exercise in which I always use food as a reward in training. Every now and then I use it to speed up a trained dog. Do not on any account give the dog the food until he is in the *exact* position in which you want him. Hold the food in your hand, tempt him when he comes up to you, and move *backwards* again, never move towards your dog until you get him in the right position. Now order him to sit, and when he does so let him have the food. Do that two or three times with a greedy dog, and he will bound straight up to you, and sit down bang in front with tail wagging, eyes and ears alert. With a less greedy dog it may not work so well, but food always helps, and cannot do any harm if used as directed.

Be careful not to allow your dog to come before he is called, as it is easy to develop a habit of getting up whenever you turn to face him. If he does come, put him back immediately, walk away from him again and turn to face him exactly as you did before. Stand facing him for a minute or so, then go back and praise him very well for having stayed sitting. Do this several times before you call him again, and try to make him understand that to walk away and turn to face him does not necessarily mean that you are going to call him.

With a difficult dog a light check cord can be useful in teaching this exercise. In teaching an easy dog there is one object in view – making him do what you want. But in teaching a difficult dog there are two – making him do what you want *and* (often much more difficult) preventing his doing what *he* wants. For the latter purpose the check cord can be extremely useful. Do not use it as a means of dragging a dog to you. Use it simply to correct the dog if he decides to go in any direction other than towards you. Reward him by tone of voice, food, etc., exactly as if you had no line.

The recall for classes B and C is incorporated in the send away, drop and recall (Chapter 11). It is simply a combination of the recall and heel free. In the early stages make every effort to praise the dog as he reaches you but progress as quickly as possible to the stage where you don't even have to look at him.

FINISH

A dog is regarded as 'finishing' when, on command, he moves from a sitting position directly in front of the handler to a sitting position at heel, by the handler's left side, ready to start the next exercise. No rules are laid down anywhere as to how this should be done. The Obedience rules say on several occasions that 'On further command the dog shall be sent to heel'. The Working Trial rules on the recall to handler say –

'afterwards going smartly to heel on command or signal; handler to await command of the Judge'.

It has always been generally accepted that the finish can be carried out in either of two ways. In one, the dog moves to the handler's right, goes round his back, and finishes up facing forward on the left. In the other, the dog 'pivots on his forehand' (to use a horsey expression), swinging his hindquarters right round to his (the dog's) right until he finishes up close to the handler's left side in the same position as before.

The first method is by far the most common, but many people think that the second looks smarter. My own opinion is that it looks smarter if done smartly, but it is not every dog that will do it that way. I have taught both methods, and have found the one as easy to teach as the other. It is also easy to teach a dog to do it both ways, or to change from one to the other, by signalling him with the right hand to go right round one's back or with the left hand to pivot round to one's left.

Some dogs appear to need no teaching of this exercise at all, while others are very slow to grasp what is wanted. Once the penny has dropped, however, it is rarely that this exercise causes any trouble, although a good deal of practice is necessary for speed and smartness.

First Method: Sit the dog facing you on a lead. Now move backwards about two paces, giving the command 'Heel', followed by a jerk on the lead with the right hand. This gets the dog on his feet, and there should be a distinct movement of the hand as you are going to use it as a signal after you have discarded the lead. Having got the dog to his feet, move forward again, at the same time bringing the dog round your back and changing the lead from your right to your left hand. When your dog comes up to your left hand, halt, and he should sit as he has been doing in ordinary heel work. Continue on these lines with the lead on, gradually reducing the backwards and forwards movements until all that is necessary is a slight movement from the right hand. Now discard the lead and continue until you can stand quite still and the dog will go smartly to heel by one command only.

If you want to teach your dog to pivot round to your left,

proceed exactly as above but hold your lead in the left hand.
When the dog has got to his feet move forward, but instead of
bringing him right round your back simply make him turn
round quickly to face the way you are going.

Some people teach this exercise with the aid of food, but I
have found that it does more harm than good, as the dog is
inclined to go right round the handler and finish up where he
started, sitting in front looking for a tit-bit.

8

Retrieving

WE now come to an exercise which may require literally no training at all or which you may find the most difficult of all to teach – depending more on your dog than on your training ability.

Most training authorities will tell you that there are two methods of teaching a dog to retrieve – he can be taught in play or by the German or forcing method. It is much more accurate, however, to say that a dog can be taught to retrieve by the German method or encouraged by play to use his natural retrieving instinct.

Whether or not the dog will ever be reliable if he is taught in play depends entirely on the strength of this instinct. In some dogs, particularly gundog breeds, the retrieving instinct is so strong that it often makes it difficult to prevent a dog picking up anything you throw. Such dogs can become quite reliable without having to resort to the rather laborious forcing method. My wife and I always attempt to teach a dog in play but, if we find that he is not going to be reliable, change to the forcing method. Usually we end up by combining both methods, the extent to which each is used depending on the dog.

We now have much clearer instructions as to how this exercise should be carried out than we did in the past.

BEGINNERS
Retrieve any article. Handlers may use their own article.

NOVICE AND CLASS A
Retrieve a dumb-bell. Handlers may use their own dumb-bells.

CLASS B AND C

Retrieve any One Article provided by the Judge but which must not be in any manner injurious to the dog (excluding food and glass). The article to be picked up easily by any breed of dog in that class and to be clearly visible to the dog. A separate similar article to be used for each dog. Test commences following Judge or Steward's words 'last command' to handler.

On top of that we have explanatory note 4:

Retrieve a Dumb-bell/Article

At the start of this exercise the dog should be sitting at the handler's side. On command the handler must throw the dumb-bell/article in the direction indicated. The dog should remain at the Sit position until the handler is ordered to send it to retrieve the dumb-bell/article. The dog should move out promptly at a smart pace to collect the dumb-bell/article cleanly. It should return with the dumb-bell/article at a smart pace and sit straight in front of the handler. On command the handler should take the dumb-bell/article from the dog. On further command the dog should be sent to heel. In classes A, B, and C the test commences on the order 'last command' to handler.

Working Trial Regulations say:

The dog should not move forward to retrieve nor deliver to hand on return until ordered by the handler on the Judge or Steward's instructions. The Retrieve should be executed at a smart pace without mouthing or playing with the object. After delivery the handler will send his dog to heel on the instructions of the Judge or Steward.

The important point for the novice to remember is that his dog must not do anything until he tells it and he must not tell it until a judge or steward tells him. Although I should hate anyone to do it to me, a judge would be quite in order to keep a dog sitting in front of the handler for half an hour before he gave the command to take the object, and, theoretically, a well-trained dog would sit still until he was told to move.

Let us first try to teach our dog in play, in other words develop the instinct which we hope is already there. Few people understand instincts, which are often confused with intelligence. Instinct could be described as an urge from within which makes a dog do something. This is due as much to his inability to resist the action as to his desire to carry it out. It has no connection whatsoever with intelligence. Instincts vary considerably in strength between different dogs and different breeds. Very often they are not apparent in young puppies but develop at some later stage. The age at which this development starts also varies tremendously. And the same applies to the speed at which it develops once it has started. All instincts are handed down from the wild dog. They may be, and often are, strengthened, weakened or modified by selective breeding and domestication but they cannot be put there or taken away. The retrieving instinct is closely associated with the hunting instinct. A gundog retrieving a pheasant to its handler is not so very different from a fox taking a duck home to its den.

The dog derives its greatest pleasures through following its instincts. It therefore finds its own reward and if allowed (it cannot be forced) becomes keener and keener. On the other hand if an instinct is not allowed to develop it will remain dormant or even die out. It is often easy to kill it outright by suppression in the early stages of development. This can be very useful, for instance, in stopping a puppy from chasing bicycles. But many people unthinkingly kill (in the seedling stage) an instinct which they later want to develop. If, therefore, your puppy brings your best hat in triumph don't scold him. Take it from him gently (it will do the hat less harm anyway), praise him *very* well, and put it out of his reach.

The age at which you start teaching the retrieve in play depends on the age at which the retrieving instinct shows signs of developing. If the puppy shows an inclination to pick up and carry objects, no harm will be done by starting when he is quite a baby – *providing* that you do play with him and never keep him at it until he is bored. Never try to force him (you can't anyhow); just encourage him if and when he feels like it.

To do this get him really excited and throw the object away from you. Something the puppy fancies is best at this stage, and throw it along the ground, not up in the air. The hunting instinct will make him chase the moving object and the retrieving instinct, if present, will make him pick it up. But it may not make him bring it back to you. Don't, on any

account, run after him. Run *away* from him and he will
probably come after you with the object in his mouth. If he
wants to hang on to it don't try to pull it out of his mouth.
Many puppies will release an object if offered food as an
alternative. This makes the puppy open his mouth, and also
serves as a reward for retrieving. If it does not work, get hold
of the puppy, place the left hand across his muzzle, and very,
very gently press his lips against his teeth with fingers and
thumb as shown in photograph 11. At the same time tell him
firmly to 'drop it', and praise very well the instant he does so.
Many dogs taught to retrieve in play spit the object out at the
feet of their handlers. To overcome this you will have to
combine this method with the forcing one and teach the dog
to hold the object in the way I shall be explaining shortly.

Remember that thousands of pet dogs with no training at
all retrieve all sorts of objects to owners who have no idea how
to train them – and they show much more enthusiasm than is
often seen in the ring. There are two reasons for this. Firstly,
like everything else the average pet dog wants to do, he does it
without suppression or control of any sort. Secondly, the dog
realizes that if he brings the object to his owner he will be
rewarded by having it thrown again. This provides him with
the pleasure of following his hunting and retrieving instincts.
They in turn will strengthen with use, sometimes to the extent
of becoming an obsession if no control is effected.

Suppose now that your puppy will not retrieve in play,
either because the retrieving instinct is too weak in the first
place or because it was not encouraged when it first showed
signs of developing. It should still be possible to teach the retrieve by the German or forcing method. Some trainers start
off on this method irrespective of whether the puppy will or
will not retrieve in play.

Don't start the German method with a young puppy. Nine
months is quite young enough even with a forward youngster,
and it has the great advantage that it can be used when the dog
is past the playful age.

The object used universally in training circles is a wooden
dumb-bell, which, for training, should be of a size and weight
appropriate to the dog. This object is used because it is so easy

for the dog to pick up and for the handler to put into the dog's mouth.

Do not start trying to teach the retrieve until you have succeeded in instilling some sort of obedience into your dog. It is useless trying to make a dog hold a dumb-bell if, at the same time, he is struggling to get away from you. Absolute obedience is unnecessary, but he must sit still and pay attention. Otherwise you are trying to teach two things at one time.

Make your dog sit in the usual position by your left side, with lead on. Now put your left hand over the dog's face, and gently press the lips against the gums with the fingers on one side and thumb on the other as already described in teaching a puppy to let go (photograph 11). This will force him to open his mouth. As he does so, give the command, 'Carry', 'Fetch' or whatever you like, and with the right hand, place the dumb-bell in the dog's mouth.

Here you are likely to come up against the first obstacle. He will almost certainly try to spit out that lump of wood. It is up to you to see that he does not succeed. In the same way as you allowed him to struggle unsuccessfully the first time he was on a lead (until he gave it up as a bad job), you must see that he allows the dumb-bell to remain in his mouth, not tomorrow or the next day, but *right now*, before you finish the exercise. Some dogs offer no resistance at all, but others require very firm treatment. At the same time be very careful not to hurt the lips or gums as this will of course make him even more resentful. Keep giving the command 'Carry' or 'Hold' in a firm commanding tone and hold his jaws shut on the dumb-bell until he stops struggling. *Immediately* he does so, change your tone of voice completely and praise him enthusiastically. And take the dumb-bell out of his mouth on command 'Drop it'.

He may have given up struggling only for a breather, and if you now try to make him hold the dumb-bell for any length of time the chances are that he will start struggling again. If he holds the dumb-bell for a split second until *you* say 'Drop it', you will have gone one step forward. But if you get him to hold it for a minute, and then he starts struggling and

8. Down. Left hand across the shoulder pushing the dog down. Right hand ready to assist the left if necessary by pulling with lead under the trainer's instep.

9. Severe correction. The dog is held firmly by the loose skin, taking care not to hurt him by pinching. The main object is to hold him in a position where he cannot avoid the direct stare of his trainer.

10. Retrieving – in play. Fun for pup and trainer.

11. Retrieving – forcing method, stage 1. Finger and thumb pressing gently but firmly on the dog's lips until he opens his mouth sufficiently to allow the dumb-bell to be placed in it.
The same action should be used in reverse to make a dog release an object he wants to hang on to.

12. Retrieving –forcing method, stage 2. Pushing the dog forward to the dumb-bell.

13. Retrieving – forcing method, stage 3. Dog on lead going towards the dumb-bell on command.

14. Retrieving – forcing method, stage 4. Dog being praised and encouraged to bring the dumb-bell. The lead is held lightly and is not being used to pull the dog in.

succeeds in spitting the dumb-bell out when *he* wants to, you will have gone several steps backwards. Continue on these lines, making the dog hold the dumb-bell for gradually longer periods. When he will allow you to put the dumb-bell in his mouth and will hold it for some appreciable time without resentment, you have reached the first stage in this exercise.

Here I might mention a method of my invention which I tried on a very stubborn three-year-old Corgi of my own. He had no intention of allowing anything to be put in his mouth and had a quite inexhaustible ability to keep on struggling. I tied the dumb-bell in his mouth like a gag, with a piece of bandage round the top of his head, rather like a bridle on a horse. I then let him 'have a go' at getting it out. After about ten minutes of trying to get rid of the thing, he gave it up as a bad job. I then told him to sit, praised him very well, took the dumb-bell out of his mouth – and we went on from there without further trouble. He was retrieving in ten days, and until his death at 11 years was quite reliable and very fast on that exercise.

Once the dog will allow you to put the dumb-bell in his mouth, and will hold it, the next stage is to get him to take it himself. Don't go on opening his mouth and shoving the dumb-bell into it indefinitely. Hold the dumb-bell just touching his lips and, with the fingers and thumb of the left hand in the same position as before, give the command 'Carry'. You may have to press the lips very gently, but if you do it properly, very soon the dog should open his mouth in anticipation of your doing so.

Very often the first indication that he is about to respond is that he licks the dumb-bell or opens his mouth very slightly. If he does, encourage him in a praising tone of voice, and he will probably take the dumb-bell, when you must praise him very well indeed. It is a good idea to finish at that point for the day or at least for that lesson.

Up to now the dumb-bell has been going to the dog: the next stage is for the dog to go forward and grasp it himself. This is done by continuing as in the preceding paragraphs, gradually holding the dumb-bell farther and farther away from the dog. At first he will stretch his neck to reach it, but very soon he will have to get up from his sitting position and move forward, which he must be encouraged to do. If he refuses to go forward, you will have to make him move by jerking him on the collar, or by pushing him with the hand at the back of his head as in photograph 12.

Continue from there until, when you hold the dumb-bell in front of you, the dog will, on command, get up from a sitting position beside you, go forward and take it from your hand. When he does, you can move back a step and he should bring it to you, so that you have now got the dog going forward for an article and bringing it back to you, which is the basis of retrieving.

The next stage is often a difficult one – getting the dog to pick up the dumb-bell off the ground. Many dogs will take an article quite cheerfully from the handler's hand even when he holds it on the ground, but take the hand away, and they won't touch it. You can encourage the dog to pick up by putting the dumb-bell on the ground and, as you give the command 'Carry', moving it slightly with the right hand or even with your toe. If this does not work, you may have to use quite a lot of force.

By now your dog should understand the command quite well. If he cannot be *persuaded* to pick up the dumb-bell you must push his head down to it and *make* him pick it up. This should not be too difficult if you have been working on the right lines. Having got the dog to go forward a few steps and pick the dumb-bell off the ground and bring it to you, the rest of this exercise is usually plain sailing.

All you have to do is to put the dumb-bell further and further forward until the dog will go right out to the end of the lead, pick it up and bring it back as in photographs 13 and 14. To make the distance a little farther you can move forward a step as he goes forward and take a step back as he comes towards you. When you can rely on his doing this – and not before – you can take the lead off, throw the dumb-bell about the same distance as you have been doing with the lead, give the command, and the dog should go forward, pick it up and bring it back. He should, in fact, *retrieve*, and you can go on gradually increasing the distance until he will go as far as you can throw the dumb-bell.

Now for the finish of the retrieve. Many very successful trainers make the dog sit in front, deliver properly and go to heel right from the start, but I do not. In teaching any exercise, I concentrate on that one exercise only, and in this case all I am concerned with is getting the dog to retrieve. If he stands up from the sit when I am putting the dumb-bell in his mouth, I do not bother. If I correct him he might well associate the correction with retrieving, not with getting up. And I never worry about his finish until he is retrieving well.

To be successful in competitions, however, finish and speed are absolutely essential, and of course speed is also essential from a practical point of view. There would be very little sense in going to all this trouble in teaching a dog to retrieve if, in the end, you could do the job more quickly yourself!

You will probably find that the dog mouths or plays with the dumb-bell when he brings it back to you. If he does, tap him under the chin with the hand, at the same time telling him firmly to 'Hold' or 'Carry'. And do not take the dumb-bell until he holds it properly. Immediately he stops mouthing it praise him well, give the command 'Drop it', and take the dumb-bell. Gradually increase the time he holds it until you have a dog that will sit and hold a dumb-bell until *you* are ready to take it and not until *he* thinks you should take it.

Many dogs are inclined to drop the dumb-bell as the handler puts his hand down to take it. This can be corrected by putting your hand under the dog's chin, as though you were going to take the dumb-bell. But instead of taking it give the command 'Carry' and make him hold it until told to 'Drop it'.

If your dog stops on the retrieve before coming right up to you, don't make the common mistake of going forward to take the dumb-bell. As I have said several times already, *never* go towards your dog; always make him come to you. If he sits wide, move backwards and keep coaxing him up until you get him exactly where you want him, sitting squarely with his head right up to you. Then, and not until then, praise him well, take the dumb-bell and finish to heel. It may be necessary to put him on a lead to get him right up to you, but it is very important for competition work.

Having got finish, you now want speed in the retrieve, which 'should be executed at a fast trot or gallop'. To do this make every effort to praise very well by actions and tone of voice at the right psychological moments. For example, you throw the dumb-bell, giving the command 'Carry' firmly. Your dog walks up to it, not very willingly, looks at it and then looks at you as if to say 'Must I?' You then give another even firmer 'Carry', and he opens his mouth to pick it up. If, at that moment, you say 'Carry, carry' in a very enthusiastic and encouraging tone, at the same time running backwards and patting your hands against your thighs, the chances are that he will pick it up and rush up to you with it. If you just stand and look stupid he will probably either mouth the dumb-bell and then come back to you without it, or pick it up and return at a slow walk, head and tail down. Not exactly what we are aiming at!

The retrieve can be speeded up considerably by playing with the dog and I always finish a retrieving lesson in that way. Having got a dog to do what we can call a 'serious' retrieve I make a great fuss of him and get him really excited. Without bothering about sitting I then throw the dumb-bell as far as I can, preferably into long grass or other cover, and let him rush off to find it. When he does I run in the opposite direction so that he will come galloping after me and I take it from him without worrying about finish.

So far I have dealt entirely with the retrieve for competitions, but as I have said I hope that many of my readers will train their dogs with a view to making them more useful. To test a dog's practical ability in retrieving, the exercises as carried out in obedience classes are quite farcical. The dog has won the title of 'man's best friend', not by being 'almost human', but by his ability to do things which man could not or would not do. An article that is 'clearly visible to the dog' is even more visible to the handler. So why does he not go and pick it up without messing about with a dog? Why in fact did he throw it away if he immediately wants to have it back? Some competition dogs would not even go to look for an article unless they saw their handler throw it.

If you want to have a useful dog, teach him to hunt for a dumb-bell and inconspicuous objects in long grass or other cover. Start by throwing them where he sees them fall but later hide them when he is out of sight. You can also encourage him to seek back for objects that you have dropped surreptitiously as you are walking along. That is of some practical value and will help to develop his sense of smell and his instinct to hunt – an instinct which should strengthen with use and make him all the keener to retrieve. The sooner you teach your dog to do this the easier it will be to teach him to search a marked area in trials. Perhaps I should put that the other way round. The longer a dog is kept retrieving clearly visible objects the more difficult it will be to encourage him to hunt for invisible objects. That may be one reason why so many dogs are so bad at the search.

9

Stand and Temperament Test

WHEN I heard that the new Obedience Regulations (1975) included a temperament test in Novice and Class A I was delighted. I had agitated for something of that sort ever since I became interested in obedience. Alas, when I read the new regulation, I found that it was not a test of temperament at all.

Temperament Test

NOVICE
To take place immediately before Heel on Lead. Dog to be on lead in the Stand position. Handler to stand by dog. Judge to approach quietly from the front and to run his hand gently down the dog's back. Judge may talk quietly to dog to reassure it. Any undue resentment, cringing, growling or snapping to be penalized. This is not a stand for examination or stay test.

CLASS A
Will take place before Heel Free. Dog to be in the Stand position and off lead. Handler to stand beside dog. Conditions as for Novice Temperament Test, except that Test will commence with order 'last command' and end with order 'test finished'. Extra commands will be penalized. This is not a stand for examination or stay test.

CLASS B
Stand two minutes, handler out of sight.

There have been many protests against this test but not for the reason for which I object. One irate enthusiast writing in the canine press said: 'Training a dog for competitions takes a long time without having to control a nervous dog for a "Stand for Examination" which serves no purpose.' This and many other statements from obedience enthusiasts (including some very successful ones) proved that these people not only owned dogs with bad temperaments, they actually condoned this weakness. But the so-called temperament test has done nothing to improve this state of affairs.

Many years ago I was asked to train an exceptionally good show dog which had bitten several judges. By the generally accepted rules of correction and reward (perhaps more correction than reward) I taught him not to bite people who handled him: just as I teach a dog not to chase cats, etc. He didn't bite judges any more but only if I was standing beside him. His temperament was in fact no better: it was merely camouflaged by training. Worse than that he was used at stud by unsuspecting breeders which resulted in more dogs with the same trait.

The advice I have given in Chapter 1 on how to choose a dog with a good temperament should be all that is necessary to help you get full marks in any temperament test. And I still advise you to avoid a nervous dog at all costs.

But having found a dog with a good temperament you will now have to train him to stand by the time you reach Novice standard instead of waiting for Class B where the dog is asked to 'Stand two minutes, handler out of sight'.

It is usually much more difficult to teach a dog to stand than to sit or down, especially if he has already been taught to sit in heel work. And, of course, we want a dog which will sit *or* stand on command.

It is usually a waste of time to fiddle about moving forward a step at a time in an effort to cajole a dog into a standing position. All the dogs we use for film and photographic purposes are taught to stand and we teach them to get up from the down. This way there is a definite action – the dog is either lying down or standing up. It also encourages the dog to stand up in his own footprints, a great advantage when you come to distant control. With the other method the dog tends to move forward all the time and can never be sure whether you want him to stand or simply to stop.

Put the lead on the dog and make him lie down in front of you. Give the command 'Stand' or 'Stand up', and, with the lead and possibly food in your hand, encourage the dog to move. As he does, gently push your toe under his flank (photograph 15). Be very gentle and, as he rises, try to put your foot right under his belly so that you can keep him from moving away from you by touching his opposite flank with your toe. In any action of this sort be careful not to push and pull the dog about mechanically. The lead and your toe must be 'alive' to encourage the dog to get up, not just to drag him into position.

Having got the dog to his feet don't keep telling him to stand. You want him to associate the command with getting to his feet. He can't get up if he is already standing! Once he is up, praise him, tell him, if you like to 'stay', but the more you repeat 'Stand' the less likely is he to associate it with actually rising to his feet.

From there go on until you can make the dog stand up on command in the same way as you have taught him his other exercises.

Some dogs don't care for the approach of a toe and tend to jump away from it. This can often be overcome by placing the dog with his side to a wall or fence so that he cannot get away. If that fails you can try my second method for which you will need a piece of string about one metre long. The lead will do if long enough. Lay this on the ground and make the dog lie down across it so that the string is under his belly. Now carefully lift both ends of the string and hold them in the left hand. Repeat the actions already described but use the string instead of your toe. As this goes round both the dog's flanks he cannot jump away from it. If, however, he is a sensitive dog he may tend to panic at the feeling of being caught by something. You will then have to be equally sensitive in your use of the string. The same applies if you have a dog which goes floppy and simply hangs like a wet rag across the string. Some people would condemn this method as mechanical. Whether or not it is mechanical depends on how it is used. Reins on a horse can be either mechanical or 'alive', depending entirely on the hands at the other end. Unless you have the sort of hand that can make a piece of string 'live' the above method won't work. It is, however, the quickest and most reliable method I know of teaching a dog to stand up.

Many people start this exercise by manhandling the dog to its feet. This often works but you still have to teach him to get up when you come to distant control. Far better therefore to teach him this right from the start. Also I like a dog that puts some enthusiasm into anything he does, including standing still. A piece of meat in the hand is far more likely to achieve this than mauling about after the fashion so often seen in the beauty ring nowadays.

Once the dog will stand, walk away from and around him (don't forget that the judge may ask you to stand '*at least* 10 paces away' in any direction he fancies) in the same way as you have done for Sit and Down.

And now you will have to teach your dog to stand for examination. Familiarity breeds contempt – or boredom – so try to get as many different people as possible to handle the dog. Training classes should be very helpful for this and I would suggest that you work on it until the dog will stand alone some distance from you to be handled by strangers. Obviously this will be much easier with a dog of sound temperament than with a nervous one. It is possible, with a lot of skill and patience, to teach a nervous one to do it too. Which is a pity as someone may use him at stud without realizing how bad his temperament really is.

When this test was introduced I suspected that some judges would dock marks if the dog moved irrespective of the sort of temperament he had. That I was right seems to have been proved by the fact that the Kennel Club has already added, 'This is not a stand for examination or stay test.'

10

Scent Discrimination

Scent Discrimination

CLASS A
Handler's scent on Judge's article. The total number of articles shall not exceed ten, all of which shall be clearly visible to the dog.

CLASS B
Handler's scent on article provided by Judge. A separate similar article to be used for each dog and the total number of articles shall not exceed ten, all of which shall be clearly visible to the dog and shall be similar to the article given to the handler. Judges must use a separate similar scent decoy or decoys for each dog. No points will be awarded if the article is given to the dog.

CLASS C
Judge's scent on piece of marked cloth. Neutral and decoy cloths to be provided by the Show Executive. The Judge shall not place his cloth in the ring himself, but it shall be placed by a steward. A separate similar piece to be used for each dog and the total number of separate similar pieces of cloth from which the dog shall discriminate shall not exceed ten. If a dog fetches or fouls a wrong article this must be replaced by a fresh article. At open air shows all scent cloths must be adequately weighted to prevent them being blown about. The method of taking scent shall be at the handler's discretion but shall not require the Judge to place his hand on or lean towards a dog. A separate similar piece of cloth approximately six inches by six inches but not more than ten inches by ten inches shall be available to be used for giving each dog the scent. Judges should use a scent decoy or decoys.

The explanatory notes on this exercise tell us:

A steward will place the scented article amongst up to a maximum of nine other articles.

In a scent test if a dog brings in a wrong article or physically fouls any article (i.e. mouths it) this article will be replaced.

90

The dog should at this time be facing away from the articles. On command the handler should bring the dog to a point indicated, give the dog scent and stand upright before sending the dog to find and retrieve the appropriate article. The dog should find the article and complete the test as for the Retrieve test. In all tests, scent articles are to be placed at least 2 and not more than 4 feet apart. Limiting the time allowed for this test is at the Judge's discretion.

CLASS A

Handler's scent on article provided by the Judge. This must not be given to the dog. In this test at least one article must be scented by someone other than the handler and must be similar for each dog. The remaining articles must be of a suitable variety in shape, size and substance.

CLASS B

Handler's scent on article provided by the Judge. All articles must be separate and similar and must not be given to the dog.

CLASS C

Judge's scent on piece of marked cloth. A decoy steward should not handle a cloth for a period longer than the Judge.

You have now come to the stage where you are asking your dog to do something which you cannot do yourself, and you therefore cannot put yourself in the dog's shoes, so to speak. Also, I am convinced that a dog that is upset and in a 'flummox' *cannot* use his nose at all well, and sometimes appears to lose the power of scent entirely. This means that you cannot force a dog to use his nose. You must always *ask* him to do so.

Before you begin, be quite certain that your dog retrieves well the article which you are going to use. Having taught the dog to retrieve a suitable article reliably, take two identical articles, one of which you have carried in your pocket for some time, the other clean and free from scent. Be careful not to contaminate the clean article with your own scent. Pick it up with a stick, pair of pliers, tongs or anything except your fingers.

Now sit the dog and let him see you place the two articles side by side and about a foot apart, a few yards from him. Go back to the dog and give him the scent from your cupped hand under his mouth so that the scent rises into his nostrils. If you just clap your hand over his nostrils he will be unable to smell anything!

With a good dog, there is no real need to give the dog the scent from your hand. Most readers will have seen dogs with no special training searching on a beach for a stone which had been held for only a few seconds by the owner. When we gave demonstrations several of our tricks were based on scent discrimination. We simply sent the dog, often from some distance from where we were standing. We could put a flag, handled by either my wife or myself, into a box and invite a member of the audience to cover it with a whole lot of other flags. Both Pip (a Corgi) and Flush (a Cocker) would pick out all the strangers' flags one at a time and drop them beside the box, then pick up the right flag and bring it back. We never touched the dogs and they could be relied on to do it indoors or out; on hot or cold days; in thunderstorms and with an audience applauding loudly.

However, it won't do any harm and may help the dog to differentiate between scent discrimination and retrieving. Having given him the scent send the dog to retrieve, using the same command as you have been using for the ordinary retrieve, as you will only muddle him by saying 'seek' or something else at this stage.

Obviously, if he picks up an article it will be either the right or the wrong one. If he picks up the right one, whether he uses his nose to find it or just picks it up by luck, praise him very well and make a great fuss of him. Take the article from him and put it back, this time about a foot beyond the article without scent, so that the dog must pass the latter to reach the right one. Send him again, and if he sniffs at the first and picks up the right one, you can be pretty sure that he is using his nose. Try two or three times, altering the position of the articles, and, if the dog does it right every time, praise very well and leave for the day.

Start next day where you left off and, if he still makes no mistakes, try two articles without scent and one with. If he obviously uses his nose and always finds the right article, then consider yourself very lucky.

Let's now suppose that you put out the two articles, the one carrying your own scent and the other clean, and the dog picks up the wrong one. Do not, as so many do, curse the dog severely, grab hold of him and make him drop it. Remember that the dog has never done this before and has no idea what you want him to do. Correction at this stage can easily put him right off scent discrimination, and probably retrieving, too, if he is sensitive or not very keen. Take the article from him the first time without praising and without scolding – just take it quietly and send him back for the right one, and praise very well when he brings it. Now try again, and this time you will be able to test the real value of having taught your dog to respond to word of command and tone of voice, as I tried to describe at the very beginning of this book. First of all, if he is a keen dog, inclined to rush off and pick up *anything*, you will have to give him the command to carry in a firm, steadying tone in an effort to get him to take his time. If he goes to pick up the wrong article you can stop him by saying 'No'. If you say 'No' in a very harsh tone, he should immediately leave whatever he is doing. In this case, he will probably leave both articles and come straight back to you. If, however, you say 'no' firmly and quietly, but not harshly, you should be able to get him to falter. This will enable you to go forward to the dog and encourage him to move forward and pick up the right article. Whenever he moves, or even looks towards the article, give him the command to carry in a very praising tone of voice, and the chances are that he will pick it up gleefully.

Some dogs, however, are very obstinate and you may have to use your own ingenuity to suit your own dog. I have had to put a lead on a dog (which became very good at scent discrimination) to prevent his grabbing the wrong article. Another idea which sometimes works is to teach a dog to retrieve a very small, inconspicuous article which he cannot immediately see, and then use two similar articles to teach discrimination. The point to remember is to encourage the dog to 'look' for the article with his nose, not his eyes. For that reason I never use a favourite 'toy' such as a glove or handkerchief, which he may recognize by sight.

From using one scented and one unscented article progress

to two unscented articles and so on, step by step, until you reach the stage where the dog will 'discriminate' a scented article among quite a lot of others. Then you can start with strangers' articles instead of the clean ones, gradually working up in the same way. You can also start teaching the dog to discriminate on as many and varied types of articles as possible, again not forgetting that retrieving comes before discrimination.

Scent discrimination on a stranger's scent is much more difficult. Like everything else, this is an exercise which should be built up *gradually*. Start the dog on your own scent and, as soon as he is reliable on that, get him on to someone else's. Training is like going up a ladder. There is no good trying to reach step No. 2 if your foot is slipping off step No. 1. At the same time don't keep him on your own scent longer than necessary. The longer you keep him on it, the more you will fix in his mind simply to find your article rather than to discriminate between a lot of articles.

When starting on a stranger's scent begin with someone the dog knows and don't change to anyone else until he will discriminate on that person's scent. We are told quite clearly that the articles for this exercise will be pieces of cloth not less than six inches square and not more than ten inches square. So you might as well use pieces of cloth in teaching this exercise. Be careful to keep them clean but if you do happen to handle one by mistake don't wash it in disinfectant or some other chemical as the dog may simply learn to avoid cloth with that smell. Fresh air and sunshine are the best scent removers but it is sometimes surprising how long scent will hold on a piece of cloth.

Start back at the beginning – never be afraid to go back to the beginning in all training. Put out one clean article and, instead of your own article, a similar one well handled by the person who has agreed to help you. And proceed from there as before. You should be able to proceed more quickly this time as the dog now knows what discrimination is. It will help to make it clearer to the dog if you use a different command with your own and a stranger's scent, for instance Seek for one and Find for the other.

When the dog will pick up your friend's article from a lot of clean ones you can add some decoys – articles handled by someone other than the 'judge'. Training classes can be very helpful for this sort of thing. Not only will you find people willing to help by placing scented cloths but you should be able to find someone who can give you first hand advice if things go wrong.

In giving the dog the stranger's scent be careful not to put your own scent on the cloth or to put your hand so that the dog will get your scent as well as the judge's. Take the cloth by the corners and hold it lightly over the dog's nose bringing the loose ends under so that the scent will rise into his nostrils. But don't suffocate him as so many people seem intent on doing! Some dogs don't like a cloth placed over their nose even if it is done carefully and, if a dog resents it, he won't get the scent from it. Accustom the dog to having this done to him *before* you do it for scent discrimination.

11

Send Away, Drop and Recall

THIS exercise is the same in classes B and C.

On command of Judge to handler, dog to be sent away in direction indicated by Judge. After the dog has been dropped, handler will call the dog to heel whilst walking where directed by Judge and both will continue forward until ordered to halt. No obstacle to be placed in path of dog. Simultaneous command and signal is permitted but as soon as the dog leaves the handler the arm must be dropped. (NB An extra command may be simultaneous command and signal, but must be penalized.)

For Working Trials instructions are combined with those for Directional Control but the Send Away instructions are as follows:

The minimum distance that the Judge shall set for the Send Away shall be 20 yards for the CD Stake and 50 yards for all other stakes. The TD and PD Stakes shall also include a redirection of a minimum of 50 yards. When the dog has reached the designated point or the Judge is satisfied that after a reasonable time the handler cannot improve the position of the dog by any further commands the dog should be stopped in either the stand, sit or down position at the discretion of the handler. At this point in the TD, or PD Stakes the Judge or Steward shall instruct the handler to redirect his dog. In all Stakes whilst the Judge should take into account the number of commands used during the exercise, importance should be placed upon the handler's ability to direct his dog to the place indicated.

The Send Away and Drop are best taught as two entirely separate exercises. The former is one of the most difficult and probably least useful of all exercises. The only practical purpose to which I have been able to put it is when working dogs in films.

There is a good deal of difference of opinion about the best

96

method to use in teaching this completely negative exercise. I think the fact that some dogs always do a perfect 'Send Away' whilst others never do is due as much to the dog itself as to the method of training. Up to now you have been doing everything you could to get your dog to come closer and closer to you, but now you want him to go away in a straight line to a point given by the judge. From the dog's point of view, you are sending him to nowhere at all for no reason whatsoever. It is because of this that so few dogs show any pleasure in this exercise. Because the exercise is so muddling to the dog it is important to remember to 'make haste slowly'.

I shall try to describe only two methods which I have found successful, although I know there are successful trainers who use other methods. For the first you will require a smooth, round post placed firmly in the ground. A garden fork pushed right home is very good, as it can be easily moved about. Now walk forwards towards the post with the dog on an ordinary lead. As you almost reach it, give him the command 'Go', at the same time encouraging him to go round the post and back to you. When he does this, praise him well. Next stand a little farther away from the post, and gradually increase the distance until the dog will, on command, go forward the full length of the lead, go round the post and come back to you.

With some dogs it is then possible to take the lead off and gradually increase the distance which you send the dog to the post. I find, however, that it is usually easier and quicker to put the dog on a long line and get him to go some distance before attempting the exercise entirely free. Put the line on the dog, make him sit, go forward yourself round the post with the line and back to the dog. Now give him the command to go and he should, by now, at least make some move to go away from you. Encourage him with the line to go right forward round the post, but on no account try to drag him away from you. If he halts or falters, order him to 'Go', at the same time jerking *lightly* on the line. When he shows the least sign of responding to this jerking, praise him very well by tone of voice.

If you take care to put the line round the post in the same direction as you started the dog on the lead, he will in all probability go round the same way. If he should go the other way round, and so wind the line round the post, it does not matter. Go up to him, praise him very well for having gone forward, and bring him back with you. From that it is just a matter of increasing the distance and of getting the dog to understand that 'Go' means to go away from you in the direction you point.

Discard the post as soon as possible, and get the dog to go as far as you can, and keep going until you call him back. Never call him back when he has decided to come back anyhow. If he turns, send him on again, and call him back when he is actually going away.

My second method of teaching the Send Away is one which I first tried in desperation with a Greyhound which I ran in Working Trials. I found it so effective that I tried it on other dogs and now always try it to start the Send Away. With a greedy dog it is quite the easiest and most pleasant method I know for both dog and handler.

Sit the dog and place a piece of food a few feet in front of him. Now tell him to 'Go', at the same time pointing to the food and encouraging him to eat it. From the dog's point of view, there is some purpose in this, and the distance the dog will go forward can usually be increased at a remarkable pace.

Once the dog understands that to 'Go' means to go forward for food that he sees me placing for him, and will go quite a long way, I start at the beginning again. I now try to make him respond to 'Go' without his having seen me place any food for him. The best way to do this is to place a piece (perhaps several pieces) of food before bringing the dog out. Be careful not to lay tracks to them or put them in a position where the dog will wind them as soon as he comes out. Throw the food away from you so that it is down wind of where the dog is going to be. And be sure to note carefully where it is lying.

Now bring the dog and sit him not too far from a piece of food so that his nose is pointing straight to it. You can place him carefully by hand and will be allowed to do so in competitions. Tell him to 'Go', at the same time pointing with the right hand in the direction of the food. Repeat this in as many different places as possible, gradually increasing the distance until he will go a long way.

The dog should now go to look for food even if there is none there. He may be somewhat disappointed at not finding any but he does understand the command 'Go'. He should also have had sufficient training to make him obedient and responsive to your wishes. Once that stage is reached it is easy to replace a request by an order. In this case, instead of asking him to go for his own benefit, you tell him to go *because you say so*. You should also be able to reward him by speaking to him in a praising tone which, to some extent, should compensate for his not finding any food. From there it is a question of practice.

Never drop your dog when teaching the Send Away, as it will encourage him to go out as far as he feels like going, and then lie down and look at you as if to say 'Is this far enough?' Simply teach him to drop on command at any time, and in any place, as any obedient dog should do. When you want him to drop on the Send Away, you can then rely on his doing so.

Many people experience difficulty in getting the dog to go exactly in the direction ordered by the judge. The safest bet is to teach the dog to go forward exactly in the direction he is facing. Whichever method you use, from the very beginning place your dog sitting facing exactly in the direction you want him to go, remembering that his body should be facing in the same direction as his head.

Now for the Drop on Command. Whether he is coming, going or just standing still, we want him to lie down where and when we tell him. In a working dog this is without a doubt the most useful and essential of all exercises. As I mentioned earlier it is the only exercise I, in common with the great majority who train sheepdogs, bother to teach a young dog before taking him among sheep.

Start by making the dog lie down beside you on a lead. Step in front of him, call him up, make a fuss of him and suddenly, but quietly, make him go down again. Practice this until the dog will get up and down quickly and happily – almost as a game. Next remove the lead and praise the dog as though you had finished the exercise. As he makes to rush off drop him quickly, call him back and make a fuss of him again. Allow the distance between you and the dog to increase until he will drop *quickly* any time you tell him. A dog taught to do this will almost certainly go down instantly on the Send Away.

Nothing in the rules says anything about the dog being sent to a 'box' in the obedience ring. Those of you, however, who have watched competitions will have noticed that this practice is almost universal. And as the rules say nothing about it judges are quite in order using the device.

For the benefit of the uninitiated the 'box' is about a metre square marked out with wooden slats stuck to the floor, or anything else the judge (not the competitor) fancies. Instead of the dog being sent to an imaginary point 'in direction indicated by judge' he is sent to this 'box' clearly marked on the floor. One result is that we now have enthusiasts 'box training' their dogs. Trainers of performing dogs use this principle and each dog has his own mark which he returns to between tricks. This usually takes the form of a stool or box but may be a mat on the floor. What it is does not matter and a 'box' as used in the obedience ring would be ideal. What matters is the fact that it is much easier to teach a dog to go to a visible mark than to an unmarked position.

So this practice can be helpful in competitions. But obedience enthusiasts get very hot under the collar when I compare obedience competitions to circus tricks! As I said earlier the Send Away is of little practical use. A sheepdog will go out to look for sheep without being taught the Send Away and the same applies to a gundog looking for game. To a policeman it could on occasion be more helpful if he could send his dog to a particular strategic spot. But not if he has to run along and place a box so that the dog knows where to go!

So far as training is concerned I would be reluctant to 'box train' any dog. It would almost certainly get quicker results for obedience classes but if you want a reliable, obedient dog I would advise teaching the dog to go in the direction indicated;

and if there happens to be a box there to lie down in it when you tell him so much the better. Don't forget that judges don't have to use this method and you might well meet one who shares my views on the subject. Also this is not done in working trials and 'box training' could spoil a dog for the Send Away and redirection in Trials.

The old Junior Stakes included 'Drop on Recall' and I think it is a great pity that this exercise is not now included in any of the Obedience or Working Trial Tests. It is without doubt one of the most useful of all exercises and I am therefore including advice on how to teach it. Many road accidents are caused by dogs rushing across a road to their owners. Most of these could be avoided (many have been) by teaching the dog to drop instantly as he approaches his handler. It is usually much more difficult to do this than to teach a dog to drop on the Send Away.

In the initial stages it may tend to slow a dog up a bit on the recall but once he knows what is expected of him he should soon regain his speed. So far you have been concentrating on one thing – getting the dog to lie down quickly. Now you command him to come to you and, when his mind and body are obeying that command, you suddenly change your mind and tell him to stop. It is not, therefore, surprising that he may not do so. That is why I never call the dog to me until he will drop instantly when he has not been called. If the dog does not drop immediately, go straight up to him quietly and quickly, take him back to where he *should* have dropped and put him down firmly. Then try again.

It is seldom indeed that a dog taught first to Drop on Command proves difficult on the Drop on Recall. If you go on monotonously trying to teach the dog to lie down when he is coming to you, you will probably end up with one which, instead of dropping, creeps miserably forwards into a lying position. By cursing him for creeping forward you will almost certainly slow him up on the recall, so that you end up with a bad recall besides a bad drop.

12

Advance Stand, Sit and Down. Distant Control

ADVANCE STAND, SIT AND DOWN

At one time a separate exercise this is now incorporated in class C heel work.

The dog shall be required to walk at heel free, and also be tested at fast and slow pace. At sometime during this test, at the discretion of the Judge, the dog shall be required, whilst walking to heel at a normal pace, to be left at the Stand, Sit and Down in any order (the order to be the same for each dog) as and when directed by the Judge. The handler shall continue forward alone, without hesitation, and continue as directed by the Judge until he reaches his dog when both shall continue forward together until halted. Heel work may include left about turns and figure-of-eight at normal and/or slow pace.

Training for this test can with advantage be started long before the dog is ready for class C as it will help to break the monotony of heel work. Having taught the dog the command 'Stand' (even if he is not yet perfect at it) start heel work in the normal way. When the dog is nicely in position to give the command 'Stand', stop slowly to see that he does it, give an extra command 'Stay' and then continue forward. Remember that he should now sit automatically when you halt suddenly so be sure to give the command 'Stand' *before* stopping. With a fair-sized dog you can bring the left hand down as you stop, run it along his ribs and into his flank. This should prevent him sitting down and obviously must be timed so that the hand reaches the flank before the dog has sat down. If he sits or moves to follow you, don't just give him another command. Go back to him quietly but quickly, prop him into a standing position and, if necessary, push him back on to the spot where you first gave him the command.

Gradually reduce the time you stop until you merely falter and eventually rely on him to stand on one command without any hesitation on your part. Teach the advanced sit and down in exactly the same way, but don't always practise them in the same order. We are after an obedient dog which does *what* you want *when* you want it, not a circus dog doing a set routine.

DISTANT CONTROL

Dog to Sit, Stand and Down at a marked place not less than ten paces from handler, in any order on command from Judge to handler. Six instructions to be given in the same order for each dog. Excessive movement i.e. more than the length of the dog in any direction by the dog, having regard to its size, will be penalized. The dog shall start the exercise with its front feet behind a designated point. No penalty for excessive movement in a forward direction shall be imposed until the back feet of the dog pass the designated point.

This exercise merely puts into practice three exercises which we have already taught. As in everything else increase the distance gradually until the dog will stand, sit or down at least twenty paces from you. Don't forget that the rule is '*not less than ten paces*'.

The commonest difficulty in teaching this exercise is to prevent the dog moving forward, especially when he stands up. The best method I have found is to start the dog on a box, table or any other suitably raised platform (photograph 16). The trouble in checking a dog for moving forward is that he may think you are checking him for getting up, the two factors being closely associated. If you put him on a box you can check him for coming off – quite a different action. If you do this from the start there is every chance he will develop the good habit of standing, sitting and lying in the same spot. And he will do it a lot more pleasantly than if you have to keep scolding him for creeping forward on each command.

13

Agility (Jumping)

NEXT to working sheepdogs, nothing gives me greater pleasure than a good jumping dog. And nothing is more pathetic than the all too frequent sight at trials of a handler trying to force a dog to jump an obstacle which it has neither the ability nor the inclination to negotiate.

Just after the war the Kennel Club passed a rule banning competitive jumping at dog shows. Many people, including myself, strongly disapproved of this action. I now believe, however, that the KC was right to ban a type of competition which, had it become popular, would have been a strong incentive to cruelty. Much rubbish is talked and written about cruelty in training. Very little cruelty is involved in *training*, and then only by a small minority of trainers. Inestimable cruelty is involved in *attempted* training.

The Kennel Club was therefore quite right to ban jumping competitions, as the desire to win would almost certainly encourage some 'trainers' to force their dogs to attempt the impossible. It is unfortunate that soon after this the KC passed a rule which in my opinion provides a far greater incentive to cruelty. I refer, of course, to the standard jumps for Working Trials which are as follows:

(a) Scale
   Dogs not exceeding 10 in. at shoulder – 3 ft.
   Dogs not exceeding 15 in. at shoulder – 4 ft.
   Dogs *exceeding* 15 in. at shoulder – 6 ft.

(b) Clear Jump
   Dogs not exceeding 10 in. at shoulder – 1 ft. 6 ins.
   Dogs not exceeding 15 in. at shoulder – 2 ft.
   Dogs *exceeding* 15 in. at shoulder – 3 ft.

(c) Long Jump
  Dogs not exceeding 10 in. at shoulder – 4 ft.
  Dogs not exceeding 15 in. at shoulder – 6 ft.
  Dogs *exceeding* 15 in. at shoulder – 9 ft.

Agility

No part of the scale or clear or long jump equipment to be traversed by a dog shall be less than three feet wide nor be in any way injurious to the dog. The tests shall be followed in a sequence agreed by the Judge and will commence with the Scale. The Scale should be a vertical wall of wooden planks and may have affixed on both sides three slats evenly distributed in the top half of the jump. The top surface of the Scale may be lightly padded. The handler should approach the Scale at a walking pace and halt four to nine feet in front of it and in his own time order the dog to scale. On reaching the other side the dog should be ordered to stay in the stand, sit or down position, the handler having previously nominated such a position to the Judge. The Judge should ensure that the dog will stay steady and may indicate to the handler where he should stand in relation to his dog and the Scale before ordering the dog to be recalled over the Scale. A dog which fails to go over the Scale at the second attempt shall be excluded from the stay and recall over the Scale. Failure in the recall over the Scale does not disqualify from marks previously gained.

The handler may either approach the clear and long jumps with the dog or send it forward or stand by the jumps and call the dog up to jump. At no time should the handler proceed beyond any part of the jumps before they have been traversed by the dog. Once the dog has cleared the obstacle he should remain on the other side under control until joined by the handler. The clear jump should be so constructed that it will be obvious if the dog has exerted more than slight pressure upon it. The rigid top bar may be fixed or rest in cups and the space below may be filled in but the filling should not project above the bottom of the top bar. Appreciable pressure exerted by the dog on the clear jump shall be considered to be a failure. Casual fouling with fore or hind legs will be penalized at the discretion of the Judge. Failure or refusal at any of the three types of jump may be followed by a second attempt and any one such failure shall be penalized by at least 50% of the marks allotted to that part of the exercise in which the dog is given a second attempt.

These must rank amongst the most unfair rules passed by any governing body. In the CD and UD Stakes a dog of fifteen inches has only to scale four feet, but his brother who grew another half-inch has to jump another two feet. In other words, a fifteen-inch dog is asked to jump 3.2 times his own height, while a fifteen-and-a-half inch dog must jump approximately 4.6 times his height. A similar rule applies to the long and clear jump and in the WD, TD and PD Stakes we have six-foot scale, three-foot clear jump and nine-foot long jump irrespective of the dog's size.

Two dogs I know were lamed in their efforts to jump the standard heights. One was a small dog trying to jump four feet, the other a rather heavily-built dog of about sixteen-inch shoulder height trying to jump six feet. Both were well-known winners in competitions and belonged to successful trainers whom I know personally. Neither is the sort who would be rough or inconsiderate in their training. But a dog cannot qualify if it fails the scale. With a dog that can jump three feet eleven inches or five feet eleven inches, there is a tremendous incentive to try to gain that extra inch.

It is not that the jumps are too high. In some cases they are very low. At the Star Dog Tournament at the White City in 1952 our dogs were first and second in the scale jumping competition at 10ft. 3 in. and 10 ft. 6 in. But one was a Greyhound and the other a Saluki – canine athletes. *And* they were fit.

What the KC Working Trial committee should decide is whether the jumps are intended to test the dog's ability to jump (in which case it should be a jumping competition) or whether they are intended to test the dog's willingness to negotiate any reasonable obstacle which he might meet. The present rule does neither. Instead it makes it difficult for many excellent dogs to qualify and impossible for them to win a stake. And some are completely ruined in the effort.

There are several practical reasons for teaching a dog to jump, one of the most common being to retrieve an object which the handler cannot reach. But the retrieve has been taken out of the scale jump. The first impression of course is that the jumps, now three in number, are a test of agility. If they were I would excuse the omission of the retrieve. But twenty per cent of the points in the scale jump are given for the dog standing still. If he is unable to stand he will not be penalized for sitting or lying down! In this 'test of agility' an automaton which does what he is told when he is told but which would never dream of doing anything *until* he is told could get full marks. At the same time a really agile dog, handicapped by lack of size, could fail completely.

Let us assume, however, that you have a dog which is capable, with training, of negotiating the jumps. Or you may just want to teach your dog to jump. A common mistake made by beginners – and some who should know better – is to base all the training on the standard jumps used at the trials. (The same mistake often applies to other exercises too.) The first and most important object is to get the dog to jump *any obstacle* on command. The more different the obstacles and the greater their variety the better chance there is of your dog tackling the jumps on the trial ground – far better than if you build jumps exactly the same as you expect to find there and never let the dog jump anything else. There is no need therefore for elaborate jumps to begin with, but later on you will require a rigid scale jump which can be raised three inches at a time.

The first and most important point to remember is to *start low*. I am certain that, as with horses, more dogs are put off jumping by being over-faced than by any other mistake. A very good guide is to have the jump low enough for the dog to see over. (Just because he scaled six feet to get out of his run yesterday don't get the idea he is going to jump six feet when you ask him today.) In photographs 17 to 20 you can see Sloopy starting on what appears to be a ridiculously low obstacle and the same dog showing what can be achieved by starting in this way.

The initial training for the scale, long and clear jump are the same. Begin with the dog on a lead and simply walk smartly up to the jump and step over it, making the dog come with you. Use the lead, not as a means of dragging the dog over the jump, but to prevent him running round it. Repeat this several times in both directions, increasing the pace until the dog will jump backwards and forwards freely and happily. Don't forget to praise well every time the dog jumps and make the whole thing an enjoyable game — much more exhausting for you than for the dog!

Next run past the jump while the dog goes over it as in

photograph 22. Note the long light line which gives the dog complete freedom but which is ready to correct him if necessary. This is of the utmost importance. There is no harm in guiding a dog into a jump with a lead, but he must have freedom *as he jumps*.

Whenever the dog is thoroughly happy on various small jumps increase the height of the scale jump a little. Just sufficient to make a definite jump and not sufficient to require any effort from the dog. If a dog *will not* do something you can correct him. To correct a dog for something he *cannot* do is downright cruelty.

Continue as before, still with the dog on a lead. Run past the jump sometimes and at others encourage him to jump over from you, turn round and jump back to you as in photograph 18. As soon as the dog is responding to your command to jump and is jumping freely you can dispense with the lead. If he runs round the jump scold him and put him back on the lead quickly and start again. Try him on as many different obstacles as you can find. But *don't* be tempted to see how high he can jump, no matter how keen he is.

You now want the dog to go ahead of you, clear the jump and stay at the other side until you tell him to come back over it. This is best taught in two parts. Start off as before but stop as you approach the jump, allowing the dog to go ahead of you. When he has landed on the other side tell him to stay, pause a moment, then go and praise well at the other side. Don't let him get into the habit of coming back round the jump for his reward.

To teach a dog to come back over a jump start with him sitting quite close to it and you on the other side, call him, giving him the command to jump and, if necessary, pat the top of the jump at the same time. Praise very well when he comes over to you. Gradually increase the distance both you and the dog are from the jump. If he attempts to run round stop him before he has done so. Scold him and put him back behind the jump, encouraging him, as in the early stages, to come over to you. Increase the distance until he will really do a recall of about twenty yards with a jump in the middle.

By combining the two exercises you should now be able to send him over the jump and call him back over it again to you. You can also make use of previous training you have given the dog. If he stops short on landing over the jump, send him away a bit further. Stop him when he has gone far enough and make him stay a second or two before calling him back. This will help to make the dog concentrate on coming back over the jump. Add to the practical value of the two exercises by sometimes making him retrieve over different obstacles. All this will tend to make the dog more biddable and is much more fun for both of you than walking about on a flat piece of ground.

We now have a dog which, on command, will jump almost any low obstacle and come back over it again. Then, and not until then, you can set about increasing the height. Here two important points to remember are that the dog is going to have to change from jumping to 'scaling', and that he is going to have to make some physical effort to get over. This physical effort varies considerably with the dog (and, of course, the height of the jump). What may require no effort at all from one dog may be quite beyond the capabilities of another *of the same breed and size*. He will have to use muscles which he has not used to any great extent before – muscles which can be gradually developed or suddenly strained and tired.

Never in the training stage ask a dog – or worse still, try to force him – to jump his maximum height. If you always have a little bit in hand today the chances are that he will make it tomorrow.

Now to the question of 'scaling' instead of jumping. This is a knack, natural to some dogs, capable of being developed in others, and one which a few just never seem able to acquire. You want a dog, which up to now has been taking a good run at his jump, to go right up to the jump, spring up to catch the top with his forefeet and pull himself over by the forelegs.

Some dogs will do this whenever the jump gets too high to clear, but others will go on clearing it until it is at their limit. When, however, you put in the board just beyond that limit, they try to clear it again. The dog then raps his knees on the top board, and may come such a cropper that he is unlikely to want to go near the jump again for some time to come – if ever!

To avoid the risk of this, start close to the jump with the dog on lead again. Take him right up to the jump, till his nose is almost touching it, and give him the command to jump. He knows this command by now, and, as the jump is very low, he should jump it, but is almost certain to jump on to the top and down the other side. Be ready to catch him should he fall back or to give a push to help him to the top.

Whenever he lands call him back, giving him the command to jump again. He should come back over to you, when, of course, you praise him very well. Start increasing the height of the jump now, and continue as above until you reach the height at which your dog cannot jump right on to the top but has to catch it with his fore-feet and scramble up. Encourage this by praising very well when the dog is actually pulling himself up and preparing to jump down.

If you have a fairly big, active dog, you will not be able to keep the lead on much after this stage. Some dogs do not start scaling until about five feet, above which height most people would have trouble with the lead.

With the smaller or less active dog, you can increase the jump gradually, keeping the lead on until you get the dog scaling the jump quite willingly and without any great effort, over and back again.

Do not forget to put some enthusiasm into your commands. Don't expect your dog to throw every ounce of energy into anything (especially jumping) if you just stand there and give him the command in a half-hearted, dull tone of voice.

From there you can gradually increase the distance you send the dog. When he lands, send him on a bit before calling him back again. If he bungles it you will have to start him closer in again until he gets the hang of it.

The jump should now be high enough to ensure that the dog must scale it but not high enough to require any great effort. Continue at this stage for some time to allow him to develop his own style. Some dogs like to rush at a jump, taking off some distance away, while others will potter up to it and take off from right in below. Let him sort this out for himself. All that concerns you is that he goes over and back again when you tell him. Increase the jump gradually so that he has to use some effort but not a great deal.

We now come to the problem of teaching the dog to negotiate the standard jumps as laid down in the Notes for Guidance of Judges and Competitors at Working Trials. Here the object is not simply to test the dog's ability by seeing if he *can* jump. Nor does it put into practice the practical purpose of jumping – to get to the other side of an obstacle. In the scale jump:

The handler should approach the Scale at walking pace, halt four to nine feet in front of it and, in his own time, order the dog to scale. On reaching the other side the dog should be ordered to stay in the Stand, Sit or Down position, the handler having previously nominated such a position to the Judge. The Judge should ensure that the dog will stay steady and may indicate to the handler where he should stand in relation to his dog and the Scale before ordering the dog to be recalled over the Scale. A dog which fails to go over the Scale at the second attempt shall be excluded from the stay and recall over the Scale. Failure to recall over the Scale does not disqualify from marks previously gained.

All of which reads like an excerpt from an Army manual. The point that stands out to me is that, not only is the dog forbidden to think for itself, the handler must not do so either. The only decisions you are allowed to make are when to send the dog after you have halted and whether to make the dog stand, sit or down after he has jumped. Some dogs drop almost instinctively (most Border Collies for example) while others prefer to stand or sit. So let your dog decide which he likes best and stick to that.

The most difficult part of this exercise (assuming that your dog *can* jump the allotted height) arises from the fact that, once over the jump, you and your dog cannot see each other. The Judge may allow you to move so that you can see the dog, and if you have a small dog you may be able to see him over the 3 ft. jump. But it is never wise to rely on help from a judge. My advice is to teach the dog to go over, stop and come back without moving from the spot.

Start this with a jump low enough to enable you to see the dog. It does not matter if he does not have to scale it. Send him on ahead of you to jump as you did to start with, gradually reducing your pace until he will jump if you 'approach the obstacle at walking pace and halt six or nine feet short of it'. When the dog will go over the jump, stay at least half a minute and come back over again, you can increase the height. By now you should be able to judge fairly well when to give the dog the command to stay. Added to this is the fact that most dogs will learn to wait until you call them back.

When the slat which obscures your view of the dog is inserted it really should not make a great deal of difference – but it very often does. It is not a good idea to poke your head around the jumps to see what the dog is up to. Some cunning ones will soon catch on to that, behaving perfectly when they can see you and doing just what they like when you are out of sight! This sort of dog can often be outwitted by making a peep hole. All that is necessary is to insert two blocks of wood about one inch thick, one at each end between two of the slats. This will form a one-inch slot through which you can see what the dog is doing. It is highly unlikely that he will see you (unless you move about) and you can scold him as he does wrong. And of course, praise him when he does right. This will give the dog the impression that you can *always* see him – a very helpful impression in training some dogs!

The obstacle for the clear jump could be a three-foot bar on two posts. The space below this 'rigid top bar' *may* 'be filled with slats, wire netting or other material'. But it may not! A dog that will jump an obstacle which he can run round or go under will almost certainly jump the same obstacle if he cannot go underneath. This sort of jump is not so difficult to teach as one might expect – provided the dog *likes* jumping. The heights, although penalizing some dogs more than others, are ridiculously low. To describe a three-foot jump as a test of agility for a German Shepherd, Dobermann or Boxer is quite farcical. Many working sheepdogs, some under fifteen inches, are expected to clear three-foot and three-foot six-inch sheep nets with no special training.

If you have not yet tried your dog over jumps which he can run under you may have to go right back to the beginning. Start with a bar so low that it is easier for the dog to go over

15. Stand. Encourage the dog to stay in the standing position by putting the foot gently under his belly.

16. Distant Control. Using a box to discourage the dog from creeping forward.

17. Scale jumping – initial stage. The jump is just high enough to prevent the dog clearing it when he starts close to it on a lead.

18. Scale jumping – initial stage. Having landed over the jump the dog is praised well and encouraged to jump back again. Note light hold on the lead so that if necessary it can be slipped through the fingers, avoiding any risk of checking the dog.

19. Scale jumping – advanced stage. The jump has been *gradually* increased from the height seen in the previous illustration.

20. Scale jumping – advanced stage.

21. The clear jump can be practised when out for a walk.

22. Long jump – initial stage. Dog on lead held very lightly so that it can be slipped through the fingers.

than under. Very gradually increase the height, and use a
good strong pole or bar of some sort. Fix it securely so that the
dog cannot knock it down if you have to *make* him jump it. A
variation of this type of jump is to make the dog jump a
walking stick, broom handle or similar object held in one
hand (photograph 21).

In trials:

*Appreciable pressure exerted by the dog on the clear jump shall be considered a
failure. Casual fouling with fore or hind legs will be penalized at the discretion of
the Judge.*

It is comparatively recently that this exercise has been
added to the Working Trial Regulations. I have been unable
to see any practical purpose in it but, just as it is possible to
teach a horse to jump even when there is no jump present, so
it is possible to teach a dog to jump over a bar which he could
easily run under. And if he really likes jumping like the little
lurcher Sloopy, both you and he can have a lot of fun.

The difficulty here is in preventing the dog using his brain
and either running under the jump or landing on top of it
thereby exerting 'appreciable pressure' with his hind legs.
This risk can be reduced once the dog will jump by adopting
different tactics from those employed in scale jumping.

The faster a dog goes at a jump the less likely he is to touch
it. You are allowed to run up with your dog in this exercise
which is a great help in egging him on. It is very easy in the
excitement of a competition (especially your first) to take a
step further than you intend. My advice to avoid this is to get
into the habit of running up with your dog and halting just as
he takes off. Pause a moment, till he lands and then join him.
The judge and spectators can then see your dog clear the
obstacle (we hope!) and there is no risk of being penalized for
being ahead of the dog.

Another method of encouraging a dog to clear an obstacle
is to place a take-off rail, as it is known in horsey circles, in
front of it. One slat of the long jump will do for this and it
should be placed approximately the same distance in front as
the height of the jump. For example if the jump is three feet
high the slat should be placed three feet in front of it. This will

encourage the dog to take off with his hind feet well behind him, reducing the risk of his touching the jump with them.

If your dog persists in landing neatly on top of a rigid low bar and taking off from there you can cheat him into believing that the bar is not rigid. Without altering the appearance fix it so that it falls at the slightest touch. When the dog lands on it he will almost certainly come a cropper. But cheating is always accompanied by risks. Next time you ask the dog to jump he will either clear it as high as he possibly can or he won't go near a jump. You will then have to go back to the beginning, so don't try this out on the day before a trial!

We are still left with the third of the 'agility tests' – the long jump. No dog should have any difficulty in negotiating the jumps appropriate to his size. If he is nearly ten or fifteen inches or well over the latter, jumps respectively of four, six and nine feet are no test of his agility. When my Corgi, Formakin Expectation, qualified CD there was only one standard long jump of nine feet. He made a gallant attempt at it, landing on top of the last slat. Another three inches and he would have cleared it, but he would not try a second time (he knew he couldn't do it) and lost all his marks, and with them the qualification CD Excellent.

In the old days the handler was not allowed to pass the first slat. The object of the exercise is to teach the dog to jump a stream or gap. There would be no great advantage in having a dog which would jump a stream if you had to go into the water to get him to do it! The old practice, therefore, was to run up to the jump, stop just before the first slat and call him back when he had landed. The new notes for guidance of competitors at Working Trials say that the handler should rejoin the dog 'as quickly as possible at the other side'. As you will be penalized if you advance ahead of the dog, I should make a habit of halting as you send him as I have already described in the clear jump.

Dogs can be taught to long jump over any sort of obstacle, but by far the best for training are slats of the type used in trials – shown in photograph 22. They can be made easily and cheaply by any handyman. Whatever you use, make quite certain that the slats, especially the end one, fall easily if the dog hits them.

As with the high jump, the important point to remember is not to see how far the dog will jump, but to get him jumping *pleasantly and willingly* on command. You should start with two or, at the most, three slats placed quite close together (about a foot apart). Now put the dog on a lead and stand with him facing the jump, about two or three yards from it. Get his attention by speaking to him, run with him towards the jump, and as he reaches it, give him the command to jump. As he jumps, either jump it yourself with him, or run close past the end of it.

If he jumps the obstacle, praise very well – but he may find an easier way by just running over the slats. If he does that, turn him round and take him back the other way. He will have great difficulty in walking over the slats if they are sloping the 'wrong' way round.

If he refuses altogether, which is unlikely, give him a sharp jerk simultaneously with the command. The great advantage of having the jump so small is that you can *make* the dog jump it. As with all training, if you finish a lesson with a dog jumping two feet, you have gone forward a step, but if you finish with the dog refusing nine feet, you have gone back several steps.

At this stage it may be necessary to keep the lead fairly short to prevent the dog from running round the jump, but, like a horse, a dog will not jump well unless he is 'given his head' as he actually jumps. Some people have difficulty if they have a dog that is inclined to 'run out'. It is necessary to steady that sort on the lead right up to the jump, but it is very important, as you give the command, to drop your hand to slacken the lead. Theoretically, a well-trained dog will follow on a slack lead, and, if he is good at heel work, he will very probably go much better that way. But some dogs don't believe in theory and if given half a chance will soon develop a habit of running out or refusing.

As soon as you possibly can, get your dog running up on a *slack* lead and passing over two or three slats. When he does this quite well, remove the lead and proceed *exactly* as before, starting off holding the collar and releasing it as you get near the jump, and go right on past.

The next stage is again to proceed exactly as before, but this time, as you reach the jump and give the command, stop dead yourself, so that you do not pass the first slat. If you wish you can stop gradually farther and farther from the jump until you can stand still and send the dog over. This probably looks better, but most dogs will put more effort into a jump if you run a bit with them, encouraging them at the same time. No points are lost for doing so in trials.

You now have a dog which, on command, will run forward and jump what can be described as a very silly jump. But he does it willingly and with a good deal of certainty. You now want to extend the jump by simply adding more slats and spreading them farther apart – *gradually*.

The snag you are most likely to come up against now is the clever dog which finds it easier to land neatly between the third and fourth slats and then jump the remaining two. The only answer I know to this is to use more slats. But some people argue that, as only five slats are used at the trials, they must train on five slats. My own experience is that a dog trained to clear nine feet over six or seven slats will clear nine feet over five slats the first time he is asked, and probably several times, before realizing that it would be easier to break the journey half way. In trials your dog has to jump *only once* to get full marks, and my advice is to get him jumping nine feet (or more if he can) really well over six or seven slats, over different jumps in different places. There is then every chance that he will jump nine feet over five slats the first time he is asked.

Some people talk of the so-called cruelty of teaching dogs to jump, and we sometimes hear people making the excuse that they will not run dogs in trials because the jumping 'ruins their shoulders'. It is not, in my opinion, cruelty to teach a dog to do anything which he is physically capable of doing, but it is very cruel to try to force him to do something of which he is physically incapable. It can be cruel, for instance, to try to force a small badly-built dog to jump four feet in trials, while a real athlete of a dog will enjoy scaling a ten- or eleven-foot jump in a competition.

Athletes, however, are not made in a day, and if you have a dog of fifteen and half to sixteen inches which will have to jump six feet, or one under twelve inches which will have to jump four feet, you will have to train him, not only in the sense normally used in this book, but also in the same sense as a Greyhound or racehorse trainer trains an animal to get him fit. Correct feeding and exercising will do far more to achieve that extra inch than constant practice over the standard jumps.

Never conclude that because a dog jumped a certain height yesterday he must be able to do it today, and that he is playing up if he does not. Dogs, like humans, have days when they do not feel quite up to scratch, although they may look perfectly well and have absolutely no symptoms of illness. They will probably do everything you want until you ask for that little bit extra, and they just cannot make it. To try to force a dog to jump, or to do anything strenuous, in these circumstances will only sour him and make him dislike the whole thing. If your dog is obviously trying, but cannot make it, reduce the jump quite a bit (so that he can jump it easily) and finish for the day on friendly terms. These remarks apply to long jumping in just the same way as to the high jump.

Many dogs are put off jumping by landing on hard ground, and I have found that most dogs with any 'go' in them like jumping up on to something, but many dislike coming down. For this reason I have a pit on both sides of my high jump, filled to a depth of about 1 foot with sawdust, and a similar one into which they land over the long jump. This means that with the high jump the take-off is soft, but that does not really matter, as one can expect them to jump higher on firm ground.

I know that in practice a criminal who scales a wall does not leave a mattress for the dog to land on, and that in trials the dogs land on the hard ground. In neither of these instances, however, has the dog to keep on jumping over and over again, as in training, and for really high jumping I always use a mattress on top of the sawdust.

14

Search and Track Back

FORTUNATELY in Working Trials the retrieve is put to some practical use.

The Companion Dog (CD) Stake Search shall contain three articles and all other Stakes shall contain four articles. In all Stakes fresh articles must be placed for each dog who must recover a minimum of two articles to qualify. As a guide the articles should be similar in size to a six-inch nail or a match box, but the Judge should choose articles in relation to the nature of the ground and the Stake which he is judging. The time allotted shall be four minutes in the CD Stake and five minutes in all other Stakes. The articles should be well handled and placed by a Steward who shall foil the ground by walking in varying directions over the area. Each competitor shall have a separate piece of land.

The CD Stake search area shall be 15 yards square, all other Stakes being 25 yards square and shall be clearly defined by a marker peg at each corner. The handler may work his dog from any position outside the area, provided that he does not enter it.

In the CD Stake a maximum five marks should be allotted for each article and a maximum five marks for style and control. In all other Stakes a maximum seven marks should be allotted for each article and a maximum seven marks for style and control.

Start as already mentioned in teaching the retrieve. Throw the dumb-bell into long grass or other cover and encourage the dog to hunt for it. Add a new command such as 'find it'. Do not use the same command that you use for starting him on a track.

The first task is to make the dog understand that, when you halt at a given spot, point in front of you and say 'find it – carry' there is an object in front of you which he *can* and *must* find – even if you have to show him where it is.

118

Next you want him to pick up strange objects dropped by strange people. First see that he retrieves strange objects handled by yourself. Then try him on the same objects handled by someone he knows and gradually get him on to complete strangers' objects. Dogs which have already been taught scent discrimination on the handler's article only may prove difficult at first and a completely different command should be used.

We must now teach the dog to stay within a specified area of 15 or 25 yards square according to the stake he is in. If a dog always finds the objects in a given area he will tend to stay within that area and, in time, is almost certain to develop a habit of not going out of it. If a young sheepdog is worked in a small area for any length of time it is very difficult to encourage him to go beyond that distance.

Although my wife and I always avoid routine in training, we did for many years have a dog act where the dogs worked to a routine. Several of our dogs went over jumps or through hoops to retrieve one dumb-bell after another, which were always placed about the same distance from the last jump. Sometimes for one reason or another I placed them a few yards further away. I have seen a dog jump the last jump, run to where he expected to find the dumb-bells, turn and come back without them. And that with dumb-bells brightly painted, lying a few yards in front of his nose. That shows just how much a dog can become a creature of habit and how accurately he can judge distance.

The reason I mention that is because, if you teach your dog to search a 15-yard square you may have difficulty encouraging him to search the perimeter of a 25-yard square. It is therefore better to teach the dog to search the area in front of you in response to commands and/or hand signals. This of course is nothing new and was the general practice amongst trainers of sheepdogs and gundogs before obedience training was heard of.

There are several ways of teaching a dog to move in different directions. It may surprise readers to learn that I know successful trainers of sheepdogs who start teaching a pup his 'sides' by tying him to the end of a long stick. The pup is given the command to move right or left and is made to move in that direction by the stick. This type of training I dislike and have never found it necessary. In anything I do or teach a dog to do I like there to be a purpose.

Assuming that your dog is obedient and keen on retrieving the easiest method I have found to teach this exercise is as follows. Sit the dog and place a dumb-bell a few yards away on either side of him. Stand facing the dog, attract his attention, and with your left arm indicate to the dog the dumb-bell on his right, or vice versa. At the same time give him the command to carry. If he brings the correct dumb-bell take it and praise him well. Now sit him in the same position and replace the dumb-bell which he has just retrieved. Indicate with the right hand that you want the dumb-bell on the dog's left. The chances are he will go for the one he has just retrieved. Stop him – not by scolding. Order him to sit or down. Try to get him to move the other way by moving in that direction yourself. You may have to move right round until the dumb-bell is between you and the dog. Eventually you should be able to make him understand that you only want the dumb-bell on the side to which you signal. In obstinate cases you can use a line to help control the dog, but, if so, be careful not to put him off retrieving.

You can now increase the distance you place the dumb-bells from the dog. With a very keen dog you will have to place them some distance away to start with. Otherwise if he decides to pick up the wrong one he will have grabbed it before you have time to stop him.

The next step is to place the dumb-bells in long grass before you bring the dog out. If you have no long grass use inconspicuous objects. Bring the dog out, sit him between the dumb-bells exactly as before, and signal him to go right or left to look for them. This can be varied by placing pieces of food and signalling the dog to find them. In his book *Gundogs: Training and Field Trials*, P. R. A. Moxon describes how to teach Spaniel pups to 'quest' in this way. And a Spaniel questing at a field trial will cover every inch of twenty-five yards square in less time than it takes the average Working Trials competitor to give his dog instructions.

Once the dog answers to right and left signals you can increase the practical value of this exercise by using three dumb-bells, one each side and one behind him. Teach him to pick up and eventually hunt for whichever dumb-bell you indicate. Be sure to make your signals quite clear. Do not signal the dog to your left with the right arm. Use both arms like a policeman on point duty. To send a dog further out, a word of command is usually easier than a hand signal.

All we want now is to put this exercise into practice. Take the dog to an area where several inconspicuous objects are hidden. To begin with it will help if you know where they are but later on it will be better if you *don't*. You will not then be tempted to help the dog or, as more often happens, to put him off by *trying* to help him. Take the dog to the area and take up your position somewhere on the upwind side. We are still training the dog and with the wind blowing the scent away from him he will have to work more carefully. In a trial I should start on the downwind side so that the wind would help him to find the articles more quickly.

Send the dog out with the command to find it. When he has gone a short distance call his name to attract his attention and, as he looks at you, signal him to right or left. As he is about to reach the edge of the allotted area call him again and signal him in the opposite direction. You are allowed to move around the area and, with a dog that will move right or left, come to you and go away, there should be no trouble in getting him to thoroughly quarter a twenty-five-yard square. Or indeed to search any area under any circumstances. My wife once lost the petrol cap of a Landrover. It hit the road and bounced onto the grass verge. Being unable to find it she went home and took Ben to the place where she had lost the cap. In a couple of minutes he had found it because he had been taught to hunt any area indicated to him instead of a square marked out by pegs. Be careful not to teach the dog simply to move backwards and forwards in response to signals and commands until he stumbles across the objects. Such a dog would get full marks for finding the objects and some judges would give it full marks for control and style. But it would not have *worked* at all. I have seen a dog practically step on an object without noticing it because he was too busy paying attention to the instructions of his handler.

It is surprising how few trial dogs are really good at this test. I believe this is because so many trainers try to teach it as an exercise instead of encouraging the dog to develop his own hunting instinct. A dog encouraged from his youth to hunt for and find hidden objects is far more likely to take to this exercise than one that has only been taught to retrieve visible objects.

TRACK BACK

Although not now included in any of the Working Trial Regulations the track back or seek back is a very useful exercise to teach. It can be good fun for both dog and trainer and can be practised any time when out for a walk. It is merely an extension to retrieving and any dog worth training will soon seek back quite long distances. The easiest way I have found to teach this is as follows. First of all get the dog retrieving reliably. When out for a walk and the dog is running free ahead of you, preferably on a path or track of some sort, drop a conspicuous article, such as a handkerchief. Walk a few yards, halt, call the dog back to you and send him for the object which he can see in front of him. When he retrieves make a great fuss of him and proceed on your walk. Now repeat the process but this time walk a bit further before sending the dog back. Continue on these lines until you can send the dog back about twenty or thirty yards for an object he can see.

Once the dog shows some enthusiasm for this game drop the object out of sight – perhaps in some long grass by the side of the path. Call him back to you and, if you give him the same command to carry exactly as before, he should use his nose to locate it. It does not require a brilliant dog to do this. When a dog cannot see an object it is as natural for him to use his nose as it is for us to put out our hand to find the door knob in the dark. If any trouble is experienced it is likely to be because the dog is not keen enough on retrieving. As soon as he will seek back for an object in response to the command to retrieve add another command such as 'Seek'. Start with 'Seek-*carry*' changing to '*S-e-e-k-carry*'.

If the dog finds the object, continue as before, increasing the distance until he will seek back quite a long way. Vary the distances you send him and make him work on crooked tracks as soon as possible. If a keen dog is always sent back on a straight track of say 200 or 300 yards he is liable to overrun completely an object left just twenty-five yards in front of him.

15

Tracking

Track

The track should be plotted on the ground to be used for the nose-work by Stewards previous to the day of commencement of the Trials. An area of ground which has had a track laid over it must not have another track laid over it until the following day. The track shall be single line and may include turns. The articles should be in keeping with the nature of the ground. There shall be a marker left by the track layer to indicate the start of the track. In the UD Stake a second marker should be left not more than 30 yards from the start to indicate the direction of the first leg.

Unless the Judge considers the dog to have lost the track beyond recovery or has run out of the time allotted for the completion of the track a handler may recast his dog at his discretion. The Judge should not at any time indicate to the handler where he should recast his dog except in exceptional circumstances.

The track shall be approximately half a mile long and should be laid as far as possible by a stranger to the dog. The article(s) should be well scented. When the judging is in progress the track layer shall be present at the side of the Judge to indicate the exact line of the track and the position of the articles.

The UD Stake track shall be not less than half an hour old and shall include one article at the end, recovery of the article not being a requirement for qualification.

The WD and PD Stake tracks shall be not less than one and a half hours old and shall include two articles one of which must be recovered to qualify.

The TD Stake track shall be not less than three hours old and shall include three articles two of which must be recovered to qualify.

In all Stakes the last article shall indicate the end of the track. No two articles should be laid together.

A spare track additional to requirements should be laid but the opportunity to run a new track should be given only in exceptional circumstances.

The area used for Tracking is out of bounds to all competitors for practice Tracks and exercise from the time of the first track and any competitor found contravening this instruction is liable to be disqualified by the Judge and/or

Stewards from participating in the Trial in accordance with the provision of Regulation No. 7(c).
   The dog must be worked on a harness and tracking line.

The first thing to remember is that tracking comes, or should come, almost as naturally to a dog as eating his dinner. The wild dog used his nose to locate his quarry and the first use to which man put the dogs he domesticated was to hunt, occasionally by sight but usually by scent. In practically all breeds of dogs the majority will use their noses – *if there is a reason to do so.*

Practically any keen Working Collie will, without any lessons in tracking, follow the line of a sheep that has strayed. The subject is not, therefore, something new-fangled – it is something the dog did before man domesticated him. The sense of smell and the instinct to hunt can, like other instincts and senses, be strengthened with use or weakened by disuse.

The first problem in tracking, therefore, is to discover what the dog wants to find, and how best to encourage him to find it. One dog may go mad to find an object which does not interest another dog at all. What may encourage one dog may put another right off. Remember that you can *make* a dog lie down, you can *make* him pick up a dumb-bell, but you cannot *make* him use his nose. All you can do is to develop the instinct to hunt and the sense of smell which are there – or at least you hope are there.

A puppy can, with advantage, be allowed to do simple tracks as soon as it shows any inclination to do so. One of the best trackers we ever had was a bitch from a home-bred litter of German Shepherds. Usually a five-week-old puppy, if it gets lost in trying to follow a person, sits down and howls. But we noticed that these puppies put their noses down and tracked – *at five weeks.* This intrigued my wife and me, so we frequently called the litter and hid where we could watch them. All seven of them would put their noses down, their tails up, and, like a pack of miniature foxhounds on a cold scent, would slowly and deliberately work the line. It was easy to hide as they became so intent on their tracking that they never saw us and if we stood still would actually bump into our feet.

In starting tracking I never use a line or other mechanical device. We are now trying to encourage a dog's natural abilities instead of subduing them as is the case in nearly all the obedience exercises. The more freedom he is allowed to use his own initiative the more initiative he will develop. The fewer instructions he is given the less inclined will he be to rely on help from his handler – a handler who in this case *cannot* do what the dog can do and unless he knows where the track was laid, is unable to give any help at all. Moreover, if he thinks he knows where the track is laid a handler may well lead his dog 'right up the garden path'!

The easiest method (and I am all for the easiest method) we have found to start a puppy tracking is to start *before* he has had any obedience training. I hold the puppy and my wife runs off and hides in some bushes, calling the puppy as she goes. I then release the pup, which will dash off to the spot where my wife disappeared. Quite often it will put its nose down and go straight to her at the very first attempt, when a great fuss is made of it. It may just rush around willy-nilly, whereupon my wife calls it again so that it can find her by sound. This is repeated, food being offered as an extra incentive for a greedy pup, until it uses its nose. It would surprise many people to see how quickly the majority of pups do use their noses when played with like this. We also reverse the process so that I do the hiding and my wife releases the puppy.

As we release the pup we give the command 'Seek' in an enthusiastic tone. As soon as it has got the idea one of us goes to hide when the puppy is not present. The other, knowing the direction in which the tracklayer has gone, takes the puppy to where the latter has left a mark by scuffing the feet. The puppy is then encouraged to 'seek', which it is almost certain to do. If not, the tracklayer, who is watching from some hiding place, will call it by name to get it started.

We continue this game (it is important to remember that it *is* a game) using as many different people as possible to lay tracks. We find children very useful for this and they enjoy it as much as the puppy. We keep only bold pups which enjoy a rough and tumble with any child, which is sufficient reward for it to go and look for the said child.

By this method the hunting instinct strengthens, making the pup keener every time he does a track in exactly the same way as it makes so many pups keener and keener to chase bicycles. We expect almost any puppy trained, or rather encouraged, by this method to do a fresh 400 or 500 yard track by the time it is four or five months old. Once it is really keen – not before – we put on a light harness and line and run behind the pup. This method of training I can thoroughly recommend to any readers who tend to be overweight! When he is quite happy with this we apply some pressure to the line and gradually slow him down to a walking pace. We don't just slow him right down in one lesson, but on each successive track over quite a long period.

From then on everything should be straightforward. It is simply a question of getting him on to the tracks of complete strangers, of increasing the distance and the length of time the track has been laid. When you have taught him to retrieve you can teach him to pick up the tracklayer's object at the end of the track or any other objects he has placed by the way.

Another method I use, usually with an older dog which has not been taught as a puppy, is based on the retrieve. This method is probably in more general use than the previous one.

Begin by teaching the dog to seek forward which, as the term implies, is not very different from the seek back. Start when the dog is fresh and make him keen by throwing an object for him to retrieve in play. Now make him sit beside you, walk forward about twenty paces and place the object where he can see it. Next retrace your steps to the dog, stand beside him and make him retrieve. Make a great fuss of him and let him run about for a bit and then start again. This time walk forward and, when the dog is watching you, place the object where he cannot see it – for instance in long grass. Be careful to walk back on the track you laid going out. When you send the dog this time it is likely that he will either put his nose down on your track or he will run to where he thinks you placed the object and start hunting for it on the wind. If he takes the latter course there is no point in going further until you get him to follow your track. Sometimes it helps if you place the object further away. Putting the dog on a lead or tracking line may help too. But don't just lead the dog to the object. You want him to lead you. Use the line just as a means to stop him hunting backwards and forwards.

When the dog is obviously following your track to the object you can gradually increase the distance and make right-angled turns in your track. You can lay a track before you bring the dog out and, instead of carefully retracing your steps, you can return by a different route. Be careful to return downwind of the track you have just laid to avoid your scent blowing back on to it, as in Figure 1 (opposite). As soon as he is fairly reliable you can get someone else to lay the track and place the object, starting with someone the dog knows and going on to complete strangers.

Scent is a big and fascinating subject. Much has been written about it and still very little is understood. The following information is for the benefit of the complete novice who may not even have seen a dog tracking.

In Working Trials 'One peg, not more than thirty yards from the commencement of the track, will be left to indicate the direction of the track'. The tracklayer starts by placing a peg at point A and then proceeds say twenty-five to thirty yards to point B where he sticks another peg in the ground (see Figure 2). He then proceeds forward in the same direction for some distance before changing direction. When the competitor brings his or her dog to the ground the judge indicates the start (point A). The handler then starts the dog off in the direction of B, and it is up to the dog to find where the tracklayer has changed direction.

It is only in films and newspapers that 'tracker dogs' take the scent from an article left by the criminal. In practice criminals do not go around leaving scarves, caps and other objects for the benefit of their pursuers! It may be known that a burglar came out of a certain door or window – he may even have left a footprint where he dropped to the ground. Or someone could have seen a man or a lost child enter a wood at a certain spot. These are only two examples of the types of clues one finds in practice. In trials the handler should imagine that the judge is a passer-by who has seen a wanted

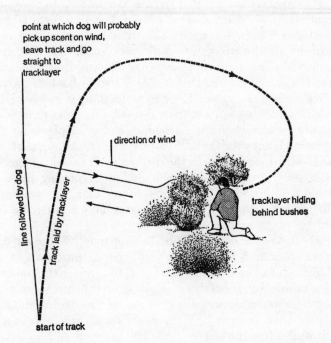

point at which dog will probably
pick up scent on wind,
leave track and go
straight to
tracklayer

line followed by dog

direction of wind

track laid by tracklayer

tracklayer hiding
behind bushes

start of track

Figure 1

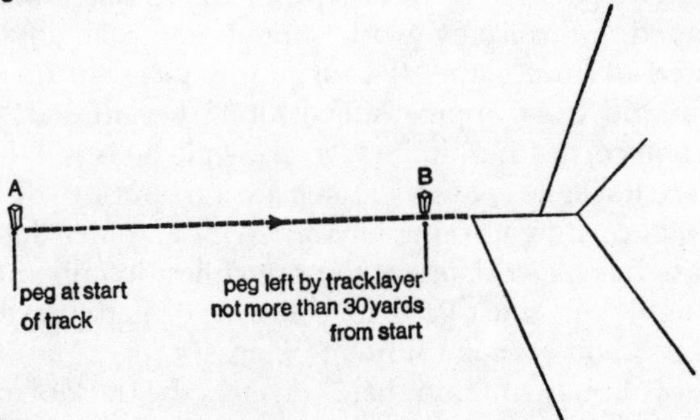

A   B

peg at start
of track

peg left by tracklayer
not more than 30 yards
from start

Figure 2

person moving from point A to point B. It is then up to the dog to follow the track until he finds the object which the tracklayer has left at the end of it.

It is an accepted fact that weather conditions affect scent in many ways. So many that we cannot deal with them all here even if we knew them all. The most important and most obvious are the strength and direction of the wind. A cross wind will blow the scent quite some distance from the actual track. It can also blow the tracklayer's scent back to the dog when he is working another part of the line as in Figure 1.

When teaching a dog to track always lay the track downwind. In other words when you go to hide or place an object see that the wind is on your back. If you lay it upwind your scent will be blown straight back to the dog who will be encouraged to hunt on the wind and discouraged from putting his nose down and tracking. And don't forget that the wind may change between your laying the track and putting the dog on.

Apart from wind direction the dog may be distracted in other ways and, although you cannot do much about the former you must do what you can about the latter. The track of a rabbit, hare, or, worst of all, deer will prove far more attractive to the average dog than that of a human being. Also many dogs will leave the line they are on when it is crossed by a fresh human track. This must be corrected and it can and often does prove to be quite a problem. To start with, any dog intended for tracking work should never at any time be allowed to hunt game. If your puppy picks up the line of a rabbit and goes yipping after it don't be amused. Get after him and correct him quite severely while he is still doing it. If you are not agile enough to catch a young puppy you will have trouble teaching tracking anyway! With an older dog it is not so easy but by working on the principles described earlier in this book you must get it into his head that everything that runs is taboo except a human being.

But you may still find that he prefers the track of an eatable rabbit to that of an uneatable human being – and who can blame him! To correct this you must do as much tracking as possible on ground that is fouled by game of any sort. And you must know exactly where the track is laid, for which reason it is usually better to lay the track yourself. Choose a calm day so that the wind does not blow the scent and you will then know exactly where the dog should be if he is tracking properly. If he now leaves the track and goes off in the wrong direction you can correct him as he does it. With a trained dog a severe scolding may be sufficient but sometimes a more direct approach may be necessary. One way of doing this is to have a fairly short lead from the harness in the left hand and another from the slip collar in the right. You can now correct him with the right hand as and when he goes wrong.

Before correcting him make *quite* sure that it is the dog and not yourself that is wrong. A remark that goes for all training. If the dog loses the scent because of an air pocket or particularly dry piece of ground he may start searching for it and leave what you know to be the line you have taken. To correct him for this can do untold harm. The real answer lies in learning to read your dog. To an experienced handler most dogs indicate quite clearly whether they have picked up a fresh track or are trying to find the old one.

16

Steadiness to Gunshot

The most appropriate occasion for testing this exercise would be in open country. The dog may be either walking at heel free or be away from the handler who must be permitted to remain within controlling distance whilst the gun is fired. Any sign of fear, aggressiveness or barking must be penalized. This test shall not be carried out without prior warning, or incorporated in any other test. The Judge will not provoke excitement by excessive display of the gun, nor shall the gun be pointed at the dog.

At one time only PD dogs were tested for gunfire and that was done by the criminal firing at the dog as it came into the attack. This meant that PD dogs associated gunfire with attacking and the trial ground became pandemonium whenever the first gun went off. It also meant that many dogs associated a gun with attack and I have known dogs who would attack anyone who even flicked a cigarette lighter. Fortunately this state of affairs does not (or at least need not) exist today when dogs are expected to ignore gunfire.

I believe there are two types of gun-shyness – hereditary or acquired. Therefore, see that you don't buy a puppy with the former and do not let it acquire the latter. There is no doubt at all that the sooner you start familiarizing your puppy to bangs and noises of all sorts the less likely he is to pay any attention to them. Puppies reared in kennels where there is more or less constant gunfire (e.g. near artillery ranges) never pay any attention to it.

Whatever you do, don't take a puppy (or worse an adult dog) which is not accustomed to gunfire and fire a twelve-bore over its head to see what happens! Oh yes! some people do that sort of thing and thousands of good dogs have been ruined by them. A cap pistol or starter's .22 blank pistol can be used and neither needs a firearm certificate. Don't forget that the crack of a cap pistol will worry some dogs a lot more than the softer though louder bang of a twelve-bore. Keep the dog with you and let someone else take the pistol at least fifty yards away. Now occupy the dog's mind by giving him something to do like playing with a ball or, if a puppy, having his dinner. When his mind is occupied get your assistant to fire the pistol *away* from the dog. If the dog pays no attention he can come close and fire again; and again; and again. The moment the dog reacts you should reassure him without making a drama of it. Your assistant should take a few steps away and, when the dog has settled, fire again. But don't continue; finish the lesson with the dog relaxed and happy. Next day start the lesson about half way between the previous day's starting and finishing points and see how near you can get without worrying him. Of course some dogs will allow the gunman to come right up and fire over them the very first time. But if your last dog was that sort do not assume that this one is too.

A dog accustomed to a wide variety of noises is less likely to be gun-shy than one brought up under quiet conditions: for instance one brought up since puppyhood in a house full of rowdy children with blaring transistors, etc., compared with one brought up by a quiet, elderly couple. When we have a puppy around we make a point of making as much noise as possible while he is playing about. We have a big rattle (football supporter's type, also used by Mounted Police) which can be used to make a loud rattling noise or clicked one cog at a time to make bangs just as loud as a cap pistol. A dustbin lid dropped on a concrete path can also make a very loud noise.

Hereditary gun-shyness I believe is often due to hyper-sensitive hearing. So sensitive in fact that any kind of explosive noise causes severe pain to the dog. I may be wrong on that theory but that is how it seems to me. What really matters is that there seems to be no cure for real gun-shyness, however caused. Once gun-shy always gun-shy; and the tendency is to get worse as the dog gets older. It is therefore worth going to a great deal of trouble to prevent it. A dog slightly apprehensive of bangs can often be gradually accustomed to them. But any 'kill or cure' efforts are almost certain to end in 'kill'.

Don't give the dog the impression that anything out of the ordinary is happening. He should regard noise as something which just happens for no reason. If he does associate it with anything it should be with something pleasant. Some gundog trainers 'call' their puppies to feed by firing a gun. With an unsure youngster this is always worth a try.

If you have a gun-sure dog don't assume that he cannot acquire gun-shyness. Several excellent guide dogs have developed gun-shyness by having fireworks thrown at them around 5 November. Some which had done several years of good work were rendered quite useless by these acts of folly.

17

Directional Control

The minimum distance that the Judge shall set for the Send Away shall be 20 yards for the CD Stake and 50 yards for all other Stakes. The TD and PD Stakes shall also include a redirection of a minimum of 50 yards. When the dog has reached the designated point or the Judge is satisfied that after a reasonable time the handler cannot improve the position of the dog by any further commands the dog should be stopped in either the Stand, Sit or Down position at the discretion of the handler. At this point in the TD or PD Stakes the Judge or Steward shall instruct the handler to redirect his dog. In all Stakes, whilst the Judge should take into account the number of commands used during the exercise, importance should be placed upon the handler's ability to direct his dog to the place indicated.

The Send Away is already dealt with in Chapter 11.

Gundogs and sheepdogs are taught directional control as a matter of course. But both have a purpose in changing direction whereas we are teaching a dog to go in the direction we want for no particular reason.

My wife and I usually teach this exercise with the help of food and many successful gundog trainers do the same. This gives the dog a purpose in going in the direction you want.

Sit the dog in a convenient place and let him see you put out two pieces of food, one to the right and one to the left of him. Now go to a position facing the dog and about five to ten yards from him. From this position encourage the dog to go for the piece of food on the right or left, whichever you say. When he has eaten one piece encourage him to go for the other one. Use a word of command (Right and Left are as good as any) and simultaneously give a clear signal to the right with the right arm and vice versa. One often sees handlers signalling a dog to the left with the right arm across the body which is very confusing for the dog. If your dog won't concentrate but simply bolts for the piece of food he fancies put him on a check cord in the early stages.

We also teach our dogs to jump up onto a box, garden seat etc. from varying distances and angles. They quickly learn to move from one to another in response to a hand signal. This is a variation of the circus trainer's system of having each animal on its own pedestal. The point is that the dog has somewhere to go instead of simply going nowhere. One need not use boxes. Mats or pieces of hardboard on the ground will do. Once he has learnt to move in various directions in response to commands and/or hand signals the 'props' can be dispensed with. Sometimes we start with the dog on a lead but with some dogs this is unnecessary.

Another method which I have seen used successfully is to work the dog along a fence or wall. Start with the dog on a lead facing the fence and send him forward. Follow at the end of the lead and, when he reaches the fence (he cannot go any further forward) encourage him to go along the fence to right or left. As soon as he gets some idea of what is wanted remove the lead. The advantage here is that the dog cannot go forward but having been taught the send away will try to go somewhere. The fence acts as a guide and prevents the dog from wandering off willy-nilly.

An old gundog trainer once showed me how he taught directional control with three tennis balls and a racket. He sat the dog some distance away facing him. Next he batted one ball straight over the dog's head. Then he hit the other two balls one to each side of him. He then sent the dog to retrieve, indicating which ball he wanted. Almost invariably the dog will go for the last ball to fall but in the initial stages is always stopped and sent for one of the others. With a keen dog he would use a line to prevent it going for the wrong ball.

As soon as the dog would go for each ball as directed he would go out without the dog, bat out the three balls or even more, then take the dog out and send him in various directions. We have tried this method with several dogs and found that they quickly learn to go in the right directions. It has the advantage that the dog is being rewarded through its instinct (the greatest reward of all) and therefore puts some enthusiasm into it. It is also an excellent test of control. The disadvantage for Working Trials could be that some dogs might tend to go out with their noses down searching for a ball.

Most people use hand signals in directional control although most dogs will just as readily respond to words of command. For sheepdog trial work hand signals are never used, although most shepherds use them in practical work. In giving hand signals remember to make them clear to an animal much nearer the ground than you. Use the right and left arms for right and left signals and never cross the arm over the body.

18

Speak and Cease Speaking on Command

Speak on Command

The Judge will control the position of the handler in relation to the dog and may require the handler to work the dog walking at heel. If the dog is not required to walk at heel, the handler may at his discretion place the dog in the Stand, Sit or Down. The dog will be ordered to speak and cease speaking on command of the Judge or Steward who may then instruct the handler to make the dog speak again. Speaking should be sustained by the dog whilst required with the minimum of commands and/or signals. Continuous and/or excessive incitement to speak shall be severely penalized. This test should not be incorporated with any other test.

All very complicated you may think and indeed it well can be, depending on the idiosyncrasies of the judge. Anyone who says this is an easy exercise to teach has trained very few dogs. Some take to it like a duck to water and indeed it is sometimes the 'cease speaking' which proves difficult. Others are difficult, if not impossible, to teach to speak on command. This is a problem we happen to know very well as we try to teach all our dogs to speak on command, with varying degrees of success. We have dogs which will bark and stop barking to a hand signal given from the other side of a TV studio. And we have others which never grasp the idea, although I daresay if it was absolutely vital they could probably be taught.

As dogs vary so much in learning this exercise I shall merely explain some of the methods we have used with success and leave it to you to adapt them to suit your circumstances. Generally speaking food is the best reward as it is easy to administer but tone of voice is equally important.

Many dogs will bark in anticipation of food and this can

sometimes be taken advantage of at feeding time. Hold his bowl in your hand and excite the dog by tone of voice. If he makes the slightest effort to bark, reward him immediately by putting down the bowl or simply giving him a piece out of it. Do not try to repeat this too often to begin with. If he barks once today and is properly rewarded he is likely to bark twice tomorrow. But if you keep on until he gets fed up he may not bark at all tomorrow. I have found that once 'the penny drops' all is plain sailing especially with a greedy dog. Use the command to speak in an exciting tone and discard the bowl as soon as he responds to this command. Otherwise he may regard the bowl as a signal to speak.

Some dogs cannot learn by this method and when it fails we try tying the dog up. This time we take advantage of the fact that most dogs will bark at another dog barking. We tie up the pupil and have a really noisy dog barking beside him. If the young dog makes the slightest attempt to speak he is rewarded immediately with food. Obviously this is not so easy if you have only one dog but you may be able to find someone to help you who has a trained dog.

Sometimes a dog can be persuaded to bark if you tie him up and pretend you are going to run away and leave him. Or simply rush around in front of him like a lunatic! Anything that will persuade him to bark at a time when you are in a position to reward him. And don't forget that you can only *persuade* him. I know of no way to *make* a dog bark.

Not all dogs will learn from the methods mentioned and you may have to use quite a lot of ingenuity. Ben, of *Training the Family Dog* television series, would not utter a sound by any of these methods. But he would bark at the arrival of a stranger or a knock on the door. So we had to make use of this. Instead of telling him to be quiet when someone arrived (usually the natural thing to do) we held him back and encouraged him to go on barking. I would knock on the door and my wife would reward him for barking. On both occasions she would give him the command to speak. When she knew I was going to knock on the door she would give him the command just before I did so. Soon he would bark in response to this command in anticipation of the knock. Once he got the idea Ben went straight ahead and became one of our most reliable 'speaking' dogs.

Once the dog gets the idea it is only a question of practice. Concentrate on getting the dog to speak on command before attempting to make him do it in a given position, whether it be standing, sitting or lying down. And get him to do it in as many different places as possible. We had a little Cavalier bitch who, in the early stages, would bark like mad in the feed house and shut up like a clam outside.

When I worked in competitions the dog had to speak in three positions, standing, sitting and lying down. But the handler could stand in front of him. Now the handler can put the dog in any position he likes but the judge can direct the handler to any position he fancies. And this can be with his back to the dog or even out of sight of him! The important points are: 1 Get the dog speaking every time you ask him and in as many different places as possible. 2 Observe whether the dog prefers to take up a standing, sitting or lying down position when he barks (very few dogs will naturally bark lying down). 3 Put him in that position and make him stay in it while he speaks. 4 Gradually move away from the dog while you give the command until he will respond when you are out of sight, have your back to him or anything else you can think of.

So far I have been dealing with dogs that have to be persuaded to bark. But many people have trouble with dogs that will not stop barking. And that in spite of the fact that one can only persuade dogs to speak while one can make him stop barking – so long as he is within range anyhow! But you don't want to cure the dog of barking altogether, you simply want him to cease speaking on command.

With a noisy dog put him on a lead and start him barking. Now give him a firm command 'quiet' which he won't obey and follow it immediately with a jerk on the slip collar. With some dogs it is necessary to jerk quite hard but do not correct more severely than is absolutely necessary. If he does not respond to a little jerk repeat the command *and* the jerk harder and harder until he does respond. Immediately praise him very well, not with food but by stroking and using a quiet, steadying tone of voice. Now repeat the process but don't make the lessons too long. If you find that, after being corrected, the dog is reluctant to speak encourage him to do so and end the lesson with him speaking. If, however, you are still having dificulty stopping him, end the lesson when the dog is quiet.

19

Manwork

Basic Training – Advanced Training for Trials

IN *Obedience Training for Dogs* I gave no advice on manwork mainly because I regard it as a very dangerous pastime for novice trainers and even more dangerous for people with whom they or their dogs come in contact!

However, I have been pleased to learn that my books are read by a lot of people whom I would not describe as novices and some have expressed disappointment that I did not deal with the subject. Added to this is the fact that I have read one or two books giving advice on teaching manwork which, if followed by either novice or experienced trainer, could be positively dangerous.

Manwork should be enjoyable to both dog and trainer but, before starting, make sure you have the right dog. A nervous dog which, without training, would run a mile if threatened with a stick can often be trained to attack quite easily. But he won't lose his nervousness. Like the dog which fights through fear he will attack, not because someone attacks him, but because he is afraid someone may do so. And a nervous animal, like a nervous person, loses his head in an emergency and becomes quite uncontrollable. No matter how well it is trained, such an animal is potentially lethal.

Probably the best manwork dog I ever had was Quiz, a black German Shepherd who was gun-shy. It was the only thing she ever showed the slightest fear of. But I believe this fear was acquired through being potted at by a trigger-happy farmer before she came to me. There was no question of her being a bit windy of bangs; she would bolt for home if a gun went off a mile away.

She took to manwork like a duck to water and immediately became very keen, so I thought I would see what she would do with a gun. At the time I had a very good young 'criminal', whom I armed with a cap pistol and told to fire it only once, when Quiz was about half way to him – and to keep on running. He ran from her and, when he was about sixty yards away, I sent her in. I had been hotting her up before I let her go and she went like a bomb. The boy fired the one round. Quiz stopped dead in her tracks and I expected her to bolt but she looked back, saw the boy still running, and went straight for him with even more enthusiasm than usual. Next time she simply faltered and then attacked quite viciously. Almost immediately she seemed to realize (this is a case where I disagree with scientists who say that dogs *never* reason) that this noise which had terrified her for so long could be silenced by attacking it. She had an absolutely super temperament but, from then on, would become really vicious if a gun was fired.

The reason I tell this story is because having taught the dog to do this there was no way of undoing it. Children could pull her about and she could be worked without any padding at all, but to anyone who fired a gun or simply had a gun in his hand she was a dangerous animal for the rest of her life.

Due to association of ideas Quiz was only afraid of gunfire and so long as no one fired a gun she was absolutely safe. But many nervous dogs are simply afraid of people and the sight of a stranger will have a similar effect on them as the sound of a gun did on Quiz. So, if you have a dog whose temperament is not quite 100 per cent don't think of teaching it manwork.

If you have a dog with a strong guarding instinct think very carefully before teaching him manwork. He may well excel at it and, under certain circumstances, could be invaluable. To a night watchman, for instance, who likes training and keeps his dog *always* under control. But in a household where people come and go and where there is not always a master in complete control of the dog it could be a very dangerous animal. A dog with a natural guarding instinct is like a loaded gun with the safety catch secured. It is unlikely to go off without any very real cause. To teach such a dog to attack is like releasing the safety catch. An accidental touch of the trigger can have tragic results.

The safest dog to teach manwork is the rollicking, happy-go-lucky fool, perhaps bought to protect yourself and your property, but, at fifteen to eighteen months of age showing little inclination to do so. Some manwork often develops the guarding instinct in this type of dog making him feel some sense of responsibility. Likewise the so called lazy dog (which in fact has too much sense to spend its life doing precision obedience stunts) will often take to manwork with enthusiasm. Unfortunately many people are under the impression that such dogs will not be very good at manwork and don't try to train them. Even more unfortunate is the fact that many people teach manwork to over-keen dogs always on their toes. They end up with a dog that is dangerous around the home and unlikely ever to win PD trials because it is so difficult to control.

BASIC TRAINING

Let us now assume that you have considered the matter very carefully and have decided to teach your dog manwork. There are two ways to encourage a dog to grab hold of a man. One in play through the hunting instinct. The other by training to develop the dog's aggressive guarding instinct. I never use the latter method and, so far as I know, all the police forces now teach their dogs by playing with them. It should be remembered that if a big strong dog like a German Shepherd sinks his teeth into a criminal's arm he (the criminal) is not going to bother too much about whether the dog is doing it for fun or in earnest!

Puppies can learn to grab hold in play at quite an early age and indeed may have to be discouraged from doing so. It is not a good idea, however, to start until the dog is at least a year old and has reached quite a high standard of obedience. Not only will you then have him under control, but you will have a much better idea than when you started as to what sort of temperament he really has. Indeed you may have decided not to teach him manwork after all!

23. Starting manwork. Playing with a sack. The dog should be encouraged to take a good hold and discouraged from holding with the front teeth as in this picture.

24. Manwork on a sack. Dog now going from handler to assistant and taking a good hold.

25. Manwork – with sack wound loosely round the arm.

26. Manwork – on an orthodox padded arm. Many dogs are reluctant to work on this type of arm until they have learned to bite properly.

27. Escorting a criminal – initial stage. Dog being encouraged to walk in correct position with the aid of the lead.

28. Search of criminal. The sort of expression likely to impress working trials judges.

29. Temperament – the first essential in a manwork dog. Dog and child are strangers to each other, and the picture was taken immediately after those in plates 26, 27, and 28.

30. Stand off and bark at criminal – initial stages. Handler encouraging dog to bark. Assistant using lead to prevent dog going in to bite.

Start by finding yourself a piece of sacking or similar material about three feet square, but depending on the size of the dog. Start when the dog is fresh and ready for a game. Roll the sacking up and shake it at the dog, doing all you can to get him to grab hold and worry it (photographs 23 and 24). Some dogs will do this right away whilst others need a lot of encouragement. When he does get hold of the sacking, keep it 'alive' without tugging it out of his mouth. Remember that, to the dog's hunting instinct, this piece of sacking is something alive which he wants to 'kill'. The more it struggles to get away the more determined will he be to 'kill' it, but when it 'dies', he will lose interest. The trouble with some people is that they never succeed in making it 'live'. In the initial stages the killing instinct may be very weak and require encouragement. If you are too rough at this stage or continually snatch the sacking away from him he may get the impression that he cannot kill it anyhow, so why bother to try? In all manwork training the dog must *always* finish up 'top dog'.

You can use a command like 'get him' (we simply use a hiss to make a dog attack) right from the start, but the most important thing is to put plenty of enthusiasm into your tone of voice and whole attitude to the game.

The first object is to get the dog to take a good hold and hang on, and nothing else should be attempted until he does. That may be the very first time you shake a sack at him or it may take several weeks of encouragement which is a very exhausting pastime! But don't keep him hanging on until *he* is exhausted. Praise him lavishly then tell him gently to 'leave', at the same time letting the sacking 'die' in your hand. If he won't leave then adopt the method described on page 79 of how to make a dog release a dumb-bell. Some dogs become overkeen and want to keep shaking the sacking even when it is lying on the ground. In all initial training a dog's natural desire to do something can be invaluable and should be encouraged to the full. But, as soon as he enjoys doing it, he must learn that it is only when *you* say so and not always when *he* wants to.

As I said the first object is to get the dog to take a good hold but the second and equally important one is to teach him to let go. Whenever the dog shows some enthusiasm in worrying the sack I find it a good idea to roll it up tight and hold one end in each hand (photograph 24). This discourages the dog from nibbling and shredding the material which is a very bad habit when you come to work on a padded arm. Make the roll big enough that the dog has a good mouthful and encourage him from the start to take it right back in his mouth.

The dog which is keen to grab hold, is usually more difficult to teach to leave and vice versa. I much prefer the former but he must be taught to leave a sack on command before he goes any further. The gentle treatment already mentioned may prove quite ineffective and it may be necessary to use quite severe correction. This is one advantage in having the dog trained to a fairly high standard before starting.

You can put your drop on command to some practical use too by giving the command 'Down' as soon as the dog has let go. You can also put the dog down, walk some distance away, turn to face him and hold the rolled up sacking out at arms' length. Keep it quite still and keep the dog lying facing you. Now simultaneously shake the sack and give the command 'get him'. When he does, let him have a good old worry and then tell him to leave and lie down.

Work on these lines until the dog will rush to grab the sacking, really worry it and then let go instantly on command. Depending on the dog you can rough him up by flapping a light piece of sacking at him once he has taken hold. Do anything which will egg him on but don't forget to relax completely whenever you tell him to leave.

By now you will know two things. Whether or not your dog will bite (quite a few never will) and whether he is under complete control. If the answer to both is in the affirmative you can proceed to the next stage. For this you can use a padded arm. But the type of arm you can buy is usually far too hard to encourage a young dog to take hold. I always start with the same piece of sacking that I have been using and simply wrap it round my lower arm. If I think the dog bites hard I put on a leather gauntlet and take the corner of the sacking in the base of my thumb and wrap it backwards round and round my hand. When I come to the end I gather a piece in my fist and told it tight, the whole effect being rather like a boxing glove. Now go through the whole proceeding as before using the padded fist instead of the rolled up sacking. If your dog really bites hard you will soon find out! – and it is then advisable to get a proper padded arm.

Once the dog will attack the padded arm on command and likewise leave on command, we come to the stage where an assistant is helpful even if not absolutely essential. My experience is that good 'criminals' are just as difficult to find as good dogs. And many of the latter are ruined by bad criminals. For this reason it is sometimes better to struggle away on one's own than have the help of a 'clever dick' who does not know what he is doing. Individual circumstances vary to such an extent that I feel all I can do here is to tell you how my wife and I teach our own dogs manwork. This is great fun for a young dog and exercises him both physically and mentally.

We never know the day we may be asked for a dog to attack, so my wife teaches nearly all our young dogs to worry a piece of sacking and leave on command exactly as I have just described. Unless there is a reason for doing so we never go beyond this stage. If we do decide to proceed further I start with the rolled up sacking exactly as my wife has been doing. Indeed a big dog, by this stage, is likely to be far too strong for most women and she would be unable to proceed further anyway. Having 'told' the dog he can play the same game with me as he has been doing with her she then takes him over and gives him the commands. I stand some distance away while she sends him in and also orders him to leave. I then wrap the sacking round my hand as already described and we start to teach the dog to catch me running away with my wife still giving the commands. Here I might mention that I have been describing how to start a keen dog, one that likes to hang on but is not very willing to let go. With a dog which is not very enthusiastic you may have to run about like an idiot when you first start with the sacking. And you can start running away with the arm much sooner. It is all a question of balance. If the dog is keen you must concentrate on teaching him to leave – mainly for safety's sake. If he is not very keen you must concentrate on teaching him to bite. Too much emphasis on leaving may put such a dog off biting.

Having done my fair share of being criminal for a wide variety of dogs at all stages of training I feel that I may be able to offer a few words of advice on those who willingly or unwillingly get involved in this pastime. I frequently 'double' for film stars who have neither the know-how nor the desire to be attacked by a dog. One very famous actor thought he would like to try it with a very safe Boxer with which he was working. But Gretel would not go for him at all and so I had to double for him.

After the scene he said, 'Why is it that this dog will attack you, her master who she obviously likes but she will not attack me, a stranger?'

'Well,' I replied, 'if you must know, it's because she does not think you are worth attacking.' So if you want to be attacked by a dog see that you make yourself worth attacking. But with an inexperienced dog make sure that he always wins.

The majority of dogs when catching something that is running away will grab the nearest part they can get hold of. So, if the criminal keeps his arm tucked in front of him when the dog is coming up behind and cannot even see it he is simply asking to be bitten on the behind. So let the dog have your arm and, once he has a good hold *pretend* you are trying to get away. The handler should tell the criminal to 'stand still' and then tell the dog to 'leave'. This is allowed in Trials and is, in fact, an extra command as the dog soon associates the 'stand still' with leaving. It is of the utmost importance that the criminal obeys the command instantly and does stand *still*. As I have said, a dog will rarely worry a dead object and if the criminal becomes quite 'dead' the majority of dogs will leave without any command at all. Likewise a good dog will attack as soon as the criminal tenses himself. There is no need to move or give any command and this is the best demonstration I know of just how perceptive a dog can be.

ADVANCED TRAINING FOR TRIALS

We now have a dog which will grab hold on command and catch a criminal running away; but if you aspire to a PD qualification you will have to sharpen him up quite a bit. That is if you still have him nicely under control and you have decided that his temperament is okay for this type of work. So let us discuss the Patrol exercises which we have not yet mentioned.

Quartering the Ground

The missing person or criminal should be protected to the minimum extent consistent with safety. He should remain motionless out of sight of the handler, but should be accessible on investigation to a dog which has winded him.

The Judge should satisfy himself that the dog has found the person and has given warning spontaneously and emphatically without being directed by the handler. Once the person has been detected and the dog has given voice, he may offer meat or other food which should be refused by the dog. If the dog ignores the food he may throw it on the ground in front of the dog. A dog which bites the person or criminal must be severely penalized.

I shall start at the end with food refusal which some dogs do instinctively while others have the greatest difficulty in resisting temptation. The easiest way to teach this exercise is to train the dog right from the start never to take food from you or anyone else until given the command to do so. And, of course, the obvious time to teach it is at feeding time. Sit the dog and put his food down in front of him, at the same time telling him to 'leave it'. If he is steady on the sit he won't move but, if he does, correct him as mildly as possible. As soon as he obviously understands to leave the food, praise him, and tell him to 'eat it up' or some such command. Lengthen the time you keep him sitting until he is quite steady. Now put the food down without telling him to sit but give him the command to leave. If he disobeys correct him again until he will stand around waiting until told to eat it.

From there you can offer him food from the hand or dropped on the ground. And you can get strangers to offer him food, first from the hand and later thrown on the ground in front of the dog. The whole object is to gradually instil into the dog that, under no circumstances, must he take food unless you tell him to do so. If he does he will be corrected more and more severely each time. Unfortunately some dogs do need very severe correction. Like humans some dogs yield to temptation much more easily than others. A greedy dog may never be really reliable while a shy feeder requires little if any correction.

I have seen trainers teach food refusal by getting as many different people as possible to offer the dog food and, as he went to take it, clip him one over the nose. And I have known dogs learn to refuse food in this way but, not surprisingly, I have also known them turn aggressive towards or shy of strangers.

An advantage of the method just described is that if, for any reason, you have to leave your dog with a stranger, e.g. in boarding kennels, he will probably eat if given the command to do so. Indeed he will probably eat anyhow as very few dogs ever become 100 per cent on food refusal in spite of many *sure* teaching methods.

A Corgi I used on demonstrations was an inveterate scrounger. If I took my eye off her for an instant in an arena she would sneak off looking for the bits and pieces invariably left by people en masse. Having been told it was a sure cure I baited a 'break back' mouse trap with a piece of meat, which I tied firmly in place. I left this lying around and let Pip out. I did not want her to get the impression that I had anything to do with it so I did not keep an eye on her. Within ten minutes of letting her out she came pottering into her kennel, quite unconcerned, carrying the sprung trap with the meat still attached and proceeded to undo it!

Now to find the hidden person and bay but not bite. Before starting I am assuming that the dog has already been taught to speak on command and has done some manwork. Start by getting someone the dog knows to go off and hide. Let the dog see him leaving but not where he is hiding. Now, with the dog on a lead, go and look for him. As soon as the dog spots your assistant both of you can encourage him to speak. Use the lead to prevent his going right up to the assistant.

Most dogs will show more enthusiasm if the criminal wears a padded arm.

On no account should the dog be allowed to bite as long as the criminal stands still. It is important to have a criminal who knows what standing still means. If he runs the dog can be allowed to go in and have a bite. Properly timed this can act as a reward for barking. We have all seen a completely untrained dog barking at a sitting cat hoping that it will run so that he can chase it. The criminal should try to copy the actions of the cat.

The criminal can now go to hide without the dog seeing him go. He should take care to hide downwind of the dog and not foul the ground over which it will be quartering. When the dog is sent to find the criminal the command should be different from that used when quartering for hidden objects. If you use an exciting 'Where is he?' as opposed to a steady 'Seek' he will learn to keep his head up when searching for a criminal and down when searching for small objects. You can, of course, use the same directional signals for both exercises.

In the initial stages there is a great advantage in having a criminal the dog knows. Indeed it may well be advantageous to act the criminal yourself and get an assistant to act as handler. If the dog does not speak when he finds you, you can encourage him to do so. If he goes in to bite while you are standing still you can correct him. The criminal should keep his instructions to a minimum, bearing in mind that the object is a dog that will work without any. When the dog works properly with someone he knows you can try him with a stranger but make sure that you find someone who will obey your instructions implicitly. And start back at the beginning with the dog on a lead which gives you much more control. This may well prove necessary as the dog will have no respect for a criminal who is a stranger.

Food Refusal

If the dog is reliable in refusing food under normal conditions as described in the first part of this chapter you should have no trouble here. Because he has something else on his mind (the possibility of a bite) he should be much more likely to refuse food. But, of course, this depends on the individual dog's priorities. For instance a keen sheepdog which has not been taught food refusal would rarely stop to pick up food while he is working. But there are others who would grab the food then carry on with the job!

Test of Courage

This is a test of courage rather than of control. Dogs will not be heavily penalized in this test for lack of control. Handlers must be prepared to have the dog tested when on the lead by an unprotected Judge or Steward and/or when off the lead by a protected Steward. The method of testing will be at the discretion of the Judge.

At last we come to an exercise which tests the inherent qualities of the dog rather than the training ability of the handler. If by this stage you find that your dog won't stand up to attack you must be a very poor judge of your own dog's character. By careful observation rather than by actual test you should have made sure of this before teaching him manwork.

This does not mean that you should go off to a trial and expect the dog to stand up to this test the very first time. You really want an experienced 'criminal' to 'attack' the dog and at the same time gradually encourage him to come forwards. A quite aggressive dog can often be completely 'squashed' by a sudden and unexpected attack from a stranger. And if he does tend to be aggressive you may, on occasion, have corrected him quite severely for it thus tending to inhibit him now. You will have to let him understand that, when you say it is okay to have a go, it is okay. If a dog is made of the right stuff you should have no problem here. If he is not you are wasting your time.

Search and Escort

The criminal will be searched by the handler with the dog off the lead at the Sit, Stand or Down. The Judge will assess whether the dog is well placed tactically and ready to defend if called to do so.

The handler will then be told to escort the prisoner(s) at least 30 yards in a certain direction, he will give at least one turn on the direction of the Judge. During the exercise the criminal will turn and attempt to overcome the handler. The dog may defend spontaneously or on command and must release the criminal at once both when he stands still or when the handler calls him off. The handler should be questioned as to his tactics in positioning the dog in both search and escort.

As you will see the above instructions are somewhat ambiguous and much is left to the personal opinion of the judge. What is not so obvious is that the dog's performance can easily be made or marred by the criminal. As I said in my advice on teaching manwork very few dogs will bite a criminal who really stands still and relaxes. But I also said that a person can appear to be standing still to a human onlooker while still being tense to the dog. This fact can make it easy or difficult to get the dog to 'release the criminal at once'.

We are not told what is the best criminal-dog-handler position in either the search or escort although the handler may be 'questioned as to his tactics in both search and escort'. Perhaps the best way would be to have an informal chat with the judge beforehand and quietly bring up the question of what he considers the best position. But that is not really practical! *The Home Office Manual on Police Dogs* says that the 'ideal position for the handler – is about six feet behind, with the dog at heel – or between the escort and the prisoner'. This is the general practice at trials. Personally I like the dog slightly ahead of me so that I can keep an eye on him and the criminal. When searching a criminal it is usual to do so from the back with the dog about four feet away facing him as in photograph 28.

You should note that the judge will 'assess whether the dog is ready to defend if called upon to do so'. Indeed an experienced trainer can assess a great deal about the whole character of the dog during these exercises. The first thing he wants to see is a dog completely under control which does not hot up when it has had a bite and which leaves immediately when told. The second thing he is looking for is a dog really on his toes and concentrating on the job.

The happy medium between these two is difficult to find and depends just as much on the dog as the trainer. My advice on how to achieve it is therefore given on the assumption that you have the right sort of dog. And apart from a good dog you will want a good criminal also completely under control yet always on his toes and concentrating on the job.

Generally speaking the best position for a dog to be during a search is Down (photograph 28). Most dogs are less likely to break from the Down than from the Stand or Sit. And most dogs can spring into action more easily from the same position. Indeed a hunting dog, fox or cat will often go Down before leaping on its prey.

You should rely on your criminal to keep the dog alert. Don't give him instructions while working as the dog will soon learn to act on them. When you are searching the criminal he must keep his eye on the dog and, if its eye or mind wanders for a second, he should either attack you or run away – or push you over *and* run away. With a slack dog he may even attack it by poking it either with a light stick or the padded arm. Earlier I mentioned a German Shepherd, Quiz, who was completely obsessed with chasing rabbits when I first had her. Apart from that any excuse for a rough and tumble was just up her street and she took to manwork like a duck to water. But as soon as she caught her man and was told to leave she would look around for rabbits to chase, often turning her back on the criminal. At the time I had a fifteen-year-old boy working for me who was a super criminal and every time Quiz turned her tail to him he grabbed hold of it. That made her mad and she very soon learnt to keep her head towards the 'enemy'. However, she still tended to look around but Pat had unusually quick reflexes and ability to concentrate. If she so much as thought of looking away he would poke her in the ribs and in the end she would 'eye' a criminal like a Border Collie does sheep.

Here we want to get right away from the 'watch me' fanatics of the obedience ring and concentrate on teaching the dog to 'watch him'! Nothing looks better than a dog which really 'eyes' his criminal all the time and this has practical advantages both for the policeman and the civilian who wants a dog for protection. The vast majority of people can be completely un-nerved, indeed terrified, by a dog (particularly a German Shepherd) staring at them. As the purpose of a police dog or civilian guard dog is to prevent people doing wrong rather than chew them up after they have done wrong this is something worth aiming for.

In teaching a dog to escort I have found it best to start with the dog on a lead slipped through the collar. If he wants to have a go while the criminal is walking quietly he can be checked and at the same time he can immediately be released if the criminal attacks you or makes a dash for freedom. Once the dog will stay in the correct position the lead can be removed. In teaching this (as in nearly all training) never work to a routine. The criminal should keep an eye on the dog as best he can and if it should relax and take its eyes off him for a second he should either bolt for it or attack the handler. The whole object is to surprise the dog. Nothing keeps dogs and people on their toes like constant surprises!

Recall from Criminal (Exercise 14(a))

The criminal, protected to the minimum extent consistent with safety, will be introduced to the handler whose dog will be free at heel. After an unheated conversation the criminal will run away. At a reasonable distance the handler will be ordered to send his dog. When the dog is approximately halfway between handler and the criminal he will be ordered to be recalled. The recall may be by whistle or voice. The criminal should continue running until the dog returns or closes. If the dog continues to run alongside the criminal the criminal should run a further ten or dozen paces to indicate this.

In spite of the long and detailed explanation this exercise boils down to straightforward obedience. If your dog sees another dog and rushes towards it you call him back. If he comes back he is obedient, if he runs on he is not. My first advice, therefore, is to teach the dog to recall under all circumstances before you start teaching manwork. If you cannot call him off a cat or a rabbit during his obedience training you are unlikely to call him off a criminal once you have taught him manwork. The mistake many people make is that, instead of making use of cats, rabbits, etc. to teach a recall they actually encourage the dog to chase them. Quiz, whom I have already mentioned, had, as I said, a mania for rabbiting but I broke her of it. It took about eighteen months and breaking was a more appropriate word than training but in the end she would recall from a rabbit which was being chased by several other dogs. She was as keen a manwork dog as I have ever had but I never had to teach her to recall from a criminal. I simply whistled and she would stop dead in her tracks and come back. During a demonstration she ran the whole length of the White City Stadium after a criminal on a bike, and when only a few feet from him stopped dead in response to my whistle and tore back to attack another criminal who had appeared behind me. And she did it in complete darkness with only spotlights on dog and criminals.

If you do have trouble with this exercise the best method of correcting it is probably with the use of a check cord. This should be about twenty-five yards long which will allow the dog to run halfway to the criminal when he is fifty yards away. Let the criminal run, send the dog and, when he is a yard or two from the end of the line, call him. Provided you are stronger than he is, the cord will do the correcting and he will probably do a spectacular somersault. Now call him back using the line as a means of correcting him should he turn back to the criminal. Never use a line as a means of dragging a dog to you, only as a means of correction should he attempt to run away. And don't forget to praise very well when the dog does return to you. To a greedy dog a piece of meat in your hand may be just as exciting as a criminal running away. Indeed it may prove more exciting – in which case don't use it! It is really a question of assessing the dog's priorities.

The recall may be by 'whistle or voice' and I strongly advise the use of a whistle. To a dog even more than a human the sound of a whistle carries much further than the human voice. And I believe that a dog in hot pursuit of anything has difficulty in hearing. Of course the saying that there are none so deaf as those who don't want to hear applies to dogs just as much as humans. But if someone calls you when you are in hot pursuit of something (probably your dog) you will not hear them nearly so well as when you are walking quietly or standing still. The same must apply to dogs. Sheepdogs are worked either to verbal commands or whistles but the one almost universal command is to stop to a whistle – usually a long high pitched blast. Indeed if one reads down a column of sheepdog advertisements one will find the phrase 'stops to whistle' recurring more often than any other.

A whistle with a high pitched tone should be used and some people use silent whistles with the tone so high that we scarcely hear it. I have experimented with this type of whistle and have no doubt that it hurts some dogs' ears. This will obviously tend to make a dog stop but it can distress those with hypersensitive hearing. In any case I like to hear what sort of a noise I am making and, being unable to whistle through my fingers, I use a shepherd's whistle with a high tone.

Pursuit and Detention of Criminal (Exercise 14(b))

The criminal (a different one for choice) and handler should be introduced as above, and the dog sent forward under the same conditions. The criminal must continue to attempt to escape and, if possible should do so through the same exit or in some vehicle once the dog has had a chance of catching up with him. The dog must be regarded as having succeeded if it clearly prevents the criminal from continuing his line of flight, either by holding him by the arm, knocking him over or close circling him till he becomes giddy. If the dog fails to make a convincing attempt to detain the criminal, it should lose any marks which it may already have obtained under exercise 14(a) or alternatively it shall not be tested on exercise 14(a) if that follows exercise 14(b).

Obviously the most convincing way for a dog to detain a criminal is to grab hold and hang on. That is the most usual practice and it is therefore the method of manwork training I have described. But it is not the most practical for police purposes. The dog which close circles a criminal making plenty of noise has many advantages over the one that hangs on in silence. Firstly he won't harm the suspect who may in the end prove to be quite innocent. Secondly he is less likely to be killed or injured by a criminal who could be wearing a padded arm. And thirdly the handler will be able to hear the dog should it follow the criminal into a wood, round a street corner or into the darkness of the night. Amongst police and service trainers one hears more and more that this is the way dogs should be trained. But very few are trained to stand off and bark, presumably because it is very difficult to teach.

In theory, it should be possible for a dog to bark round a criminal without biting until told to go in by the handler. I have seen some dogs which would do it beautifully. But dogs which can be taught this, not to mention trainers who can teach them, are few and far between. My opinion therefore is that it will be some time before it becomes general practice at trials.

Stand off and bark at a criminal

To teach a dog to stand off and bark without biting, start by finding a hidden criminal and barking on command as you did when teaching the dog to quarter. When he is good at this exercise enlist the help of a capable and fairly strong assistant (additional to the criminal) who will have the dog on a long lead. Your job is now to encourage the dog to bark at the criminal and at the same time discourage it from going in and having a bite. Your assistant will by means of the lead prevent the dog from getting too close and if it really tries to bite he can correct it with the lead. He should not, however, utter any words of command or correction. You are the handler and he is merely the anchor man (photograph 30).

The criminal should keep turning to face the dog which should be encouraged to run round and round. If he flicks at the dog with a light switch it will be prevented from biting in retaliation and should soon learn to keep just out of reach of the stick.

Before starting this exercise make sure that both your assistant and criminal know what is expected of them. You want to be able to concentrate on the dog and if it really does make a noise they won't hear you anyhow!

20

Agility Tests

SOON after the last revision of this book in 1977 a new dog sport emerged in the form of Agility Tests. These have proved tremendously popular with both competitors and the general public. Apart from sheepdog trials it is the only dog activity which has caught the imagination of television producers and that alone ensures the sport's progress in the future.

My only regret about Agility Tests is that they did not come into existence twenty years ago when I was more active and competitive than I am today. In fact several of the obstacles used in these tests are very similar to those we used when we had a team of demonstration dogs. Our dog walk was 4 in. wide and 7 ft. 6 in. from the ground and we had several dogs which scaled 10 ft. and more over a perpendicular jump – which does not mean that I think such obstacles should be used in competitive agility tests.

Kennel Club Regulations for Agility Tests were first published in July 1983 and it is pretty certain that there will be many amendments and additions to these rules as happens with all new sports. In its regulations the Kennel Club says 'Agility Tests are considered to be a "fun" type competition designed for spectator appeal.' I cannot recollect having seen the word 'fun' in any Kennel Club document before and hope there is no significance in the fact that it is in inverted commas!

The rules on 'Standard Marking' are somewhat brief: '5 faults for each failure to negotiate any obstacle correctly. Failure to complete the course correctly – disqualified'. One can assume that the 5 faults means 5 seconds added to the total time but what is not at all clear is the word 'correctly' which is mentioned twice in the above two lines. As I said it is likely that the rules will be amended at some time and it may be that more details will be given as to what is correct. Unfortunately, little can be done about individual judges' interpretation of the rules. The explanatory notes for Obedience Tests still say that 'the dog should work in a happy and natural manner.' One has only to watch an advanced obedience class in action to realize that the average judge has very peculiar ideas about what is natural.

Let's hope that a similar state of affairs does not creep into Agility Tests. Organizers, I hope, will not forget that three-lettered word 'fun'. Fun for the spectators as well as the competitor – and of course not forgetting the dog. They must not forget either that the main source of excitement to the spectator arises from the seconds ticking away on the clock. And this is in no way affected by a judge's interpretation. By all means devise tests which will ensure that the dog which is under complete control has the advantage over one that races willy nilly round the course at record speed. But don't forget that it is the latter which will get most applause from the audience. If Agility Tests are to continue to increase in popularity with competitors and spectators, the emphasis should be as much as possible on the clock and as little as possible on personal opinions and idiosyncrasies of judges.

Although I have not trained dogs specifically for Agility Tests I have trained dogs to do most of the exercises involved in these tests. We simply teach our dogs to be obedient and if a film director suddenly wants a dog to cross a plank or go through a tunnel I would expect to teach almost any dog to negotiate either obstacle with very little trouble. I say almost any dog as some dogs have a phobia about heights and some don't like the dark. Which brings us right back to square one when I said that the first essential to successful training is finding the right dog for the job in mind.

Having found the right dog, or one you think is suitable for agility I would suggest that first of all you teach him to be obedient. Precision heel work is not essential but he must go with you on a slack lead and without a lead. And it will help if he walks on either side. All our own dogs are taught to lead on both hands which is quite easy provided it is done before the dog develops a habit of always being on the left. The other exercises I have described which are necessary for Agility Tests are the Down, Send Away, Drop and Recall and Directional Control. You should also start him jumping as described in Chapter 13 on Agility. Even more important is to teach him to negotiate any obstacles which come to hand – a seat in the park, a fallen tree, walls, ditches, anything you can find. Peter Lewis has written a book called *The Agility Dog* (Canine Publications) which gives much valuable advice based on first-hand experience. But he makes it all sound such hard work that I feel it could put some people off agility training altogether. However, I do advise anyone interested in this new sport to read this book.

At one of the Olympia Horse Shows where the Agility Stakes were staged, they had an extra competition for celebrities with their own or borrowed dogs. One of these was Jennie Loriston-Clarke, our leading dressage rider, with her lurcher, Foxy, who successfully negotiated every obstacle. Their time was not so fast as the others but this dog had never seen a dog walk, a seesaw or a tunnel until he went into the arena to compete. He has never had any obedience training as seen at classes and I am sure would be quite horrified at the idea of doing heel work. But Jennie plays with him over show jumps, field gates, streams, fallen trees etc. etc. so that when she points to something and says 'hup' he jumps – just for fun. With very little practice Foxy could hold his own with the best in Agility Tests.

If you intend competing in Agility Tests it is virtually essential to join a club. (The Kennel Club will have the names of clubs in your area.) Here you will be able to use the type of equipment that is used in competitions and you will be able to get advice from those who have been successful in competitions. As an added bonus you will almost certainly make new friends who, like you, want to have fun with their dogs. But don't confine your training to once a week sessions at a class. Combine training with exercise so that when you point to something and tell the dog to jump, he jumps and if you shout 'down' when he is 50 yards away he drops instantly.

That way you won't have to worry about encountering some strange obstacle when you enter the competition arena.

21

Handling in Competitions

So far our object has been to achieve as near as possible perfect behaviour by the dog. This book would not be complete, however, without some remarks on the correct behaviour of the handler.

Although my remarks are directed to competitors in Obedience Classes they also apply to Trials and Agility Tests. Most people will agree that the atmosphere at the last two are less tense (dare I say more friendly?) and if you can cope with Obedience Classes you should have little trouble with the other two.

To start with I should advise you to go along as a spectator to as many competitions as you possibly can. Watch carefully the behaviour of dogs and handlers, particularly the successful ones.

Next, try to attend some training classes, where you will be able to work your dog under strange conditions and someone with more experience than yourself will be able to criticize your mistakes. If this is impossible, try to find someone or, better still, several people who are keen on training, and work your dogs together, even if you have no expert instructor.

There are occasions when the latter may be the better course. As I have said before, training classes are only as good as their instructors. There are many excellent instructors who give their valuable time and knowledge free to help those less experienced than themselves. We should all be grateful to these people (I certainly was in my early days of training) but don't assume that because someone has trained his own dog to become an obedience champion this automatically means that he knows how to train yours.

I am assuming that you have familiarized your dog with as many distractions as possible ever since you had him. Take him out and work him in as many strange places as possible, but use a little commonsense in the choice of venues. If someone accidentally steps on the dog it will undo any possible good. If care is taken to avoid this, any public park or village green, with its dozens of uncontrolled mongrels roaming around and children playing football, is usually a good place for some of the training.

Let us assume that your dog will do all the Class A exercises in various places and with various distractions and you decide to enter him in his (and your) first competition. *Do not* enter him in Class A. Enter him in Pre-beginners or Beginners. You will then be able to give him all the encouragement you like, and you will not have to leave him out of sight.

As the day of the Competition approaches do not be carried away by your enthusiasm and train, train, train, until, by the time the day arrives, the dog is thoroughly stale. If you have carefully studied your dog throughout his training, you should, by now, have a fair idea of how much work he requires to keep him nicely under control. If he is the type of dog that does everything he is asked, but very soon shows signs of getting fed up with it, give him as little work as possible. If, on the other hand, he appears to forget everything each time he misses a day's training, you will have to keep at him.

Whatever type of dog you have, do not have a sudden attack of 'training fever'. Just carry on along the lines that you have found obtain best results, up to two days before the competition. Unless you have a very keen, headstrong dog, do not do *any* training at all the day before the event.

The great day has now arrived, and we hope that you and your dog are fighting fit. I say 'you and your dog' because, although I have dealt at considerable length with temperament in the dog, and have said very little about temperament in the handler, I am certain that far more first attempt failures are due to the handlers going to pieces than to any fault in the dogs. People who have seen me work my dogs in public may find it hard to believe that I should ever have suffered from nerves. But I have, on many occasions, one of which stands out clearly in my mind.

My first public appearance with a dog was at the age of eighteen when I entered a young bitch, Floss, in a local sheepdog trial. She was the first dog I had ever trained from scratch (from well behind scratch, thanks to my father's efforts before I took her over!) and one of the best I have ever owned. The competitors drew for order of running and I had no beginner's luck. I drew to run first!

In sheepdog trials a post is usually driven in the ground from which the competitor starts his dog, himself staying within a certain distance of the post. Although quite a small trial, it was held near Crieff during the holiday season and there was an audience of 5,000. From the ringside the post did not seem far away. By the time I reached it I felt as though I had walked miles!

The sheep were let out about 600 yards away out of sight of the dog. I sent Floss out but she did not see the sheep until she was quite close to them. Finding them suddenly, she went down on the spot without any command and the sheep turned to face her. Now Floss had her failings and I knew that, if I were not careful, she was liable to whip in and bring three sheep 600 yards in record time! I wanted her to 'lift' them very gently and my command to come on is a low whistle. So I tried to whistle in a nice steady tone. But to my horror I couldn't whistle at all! All that came from my lips resembled a very feeble attempt to blow out a candle. And the dog was 600 yards away, not just across the ring as yours is likely to be.

Yes, I know very well what beginner's nerves are like. Having overcome them to the extent of now being officially classed as a showman, I hope I may be able to help you to overcome yours – if you have any.

First of all remember that the experts of today were the novices of yesterday. If, therefore, your performance is not quite what you would like, the experts are much more likely to sympathize with you than to ridicule you. Anyone who says he or she has never been let down by a dog is either a liar or has trained remarkably few dogs!

Remember too that even if the judge thinks very little of

your dog's performance there may be a lot of ringside spectators who think he is wonderful.

You may have noticed competitors practising all the exercises before they enter the ring. As these include many of the most successful trainers, the novice, naturally, thinks that this must be the thing to do. What he or she overlooks is that many of these experts train dogs which the average novice could not handle at all.

I am referring to the very hard, boisterous type, whose handler has to keep on top all the time and who must, therefore, keep on working the dog right up to the time he enters the ring. It is fortunate that all dogs do not belong to this class, and I am certain that there are far more novices who ruin their chances of success by practising beforehand than there are those who improve them.

One can see at any show handlers, not all novices, taking their dogs out to practice beforehand, starting off with really good heel work and entering the ring with a dog which is fed up with the whole proceeding.

To avoid this, study your own individual dog and don't worry what other people do with theirs. If you have a hard, wilful dog, keep him with you as much as you can, take him round the rings, catch him out several times by giving him a sharp jerk when his mind is wandering, do some heel work, Sits and Downs. By the time he goes into the ring you can hope that he has settled down and is prepared to do what you want, without too much argument.

If, on the other hand, you have a dog that very soon gets slow and loses interest you will have to treat him very differently. First of all, never forget to take him out to run loose and relieve himself thoroughly just when your class has started or is about to start (depending on how many entries there are). That, of course, applies to the former type of dog, too. Now put him back on his bench and go round to see what is happening in the ring.

Perhaps you have a rather lazy dog. If so, leave him on his bench till the last minute, especially if the weather is hot. Wait by the ring until the dog before you has done some of his exercises. If your bench is near the ring, you can wait until he is ready to do the retrieve, the last of his exercises, but remember that it is your responsibility, not the Steward's, to see that you are in the ring on time. Then rush to your bench, take your dog off quickly, giving him the impression that something terrific is going to happen, and rush back to the ring. If the dog before you has not quite finished, do some smart about-turns and halts, and always go into the ring quickly, doing one or two sharp halts, with a good jerk if necessary, on your way. That will impress on the dog that he is not just out for a stroll, but is expected to jump to it. It will have a far more beneficial effect on the average dog than constant practising beforehand.

The majority of dogs, I think, fall between the two extremes I have just tried to describe, and it is up to you to study your own dog to find out how he works best.

Once in the ring you are under judge's orders. Listen carefully to what he tells you. If there are points not quite clear, especially if this is your first attempt, *ask the judge before you start*. Don't be afraid it will make you look silly. You will not look half so silly as if you misunderstand and do the wrong thing!

There will also be one or two stewards whom the judge may ask to pass on instructions to you. Remember that a steward's job is to help the judge *and* the competitors. He or she is therefore merely doing his or her duty, not doing you a favour, in answering any queries you may have. Concentrate on your dog, the judge and/or stewards – *ignore everyone and everything else*.

Besides doing everything the judge or steward tells you, be careful not to do anything *until* you are told. For example, in the Retrieve do not throw your dumb-bell or send your dog, or take your dumb-bell or make the dog finish to heel *until you are told to do so*.

The commands in heel work are quite simple – Forward; Right Turn; Left Turn; About Turn and Halt. These are all, until you come to the more advanced 'double' and 'slow' paces. Nothing could be simpler than that – but it is quite amazing the number of handlers at training and obedience classes who do not appear to know right from left!

Do try to practise until you know without having to think, as it is very hard on a judge to have to penalize an obviously good dog because of the handler's stupidity!

About-turns are always to the right, and the right and left turns should be right-angled turns, not just a slovenly half-circled wander round the corner.

And don't forget that when the judge says forward, you keep going forward until he stops you. If he forgets to do so and you walk into the ropes it is he who will look a fool, not you!

Don't get upset because the judge or steward shouts his commands at you. If he did not, you might not hear, and that would be worse.

Perhaps I should have emphasized earlier the importance of studying the latest Kennel Club Rules and Regulations and also any further instructions contained in the schedule of the particular show. This should be done *before* you make your entry and, unless you have a better memory than I have, do some revision before the show. Once you have actually competed you will find rules and regulations easy to understand and remember, but if there is anything you do not understand to begin with, ask someone who does – before you make any mistakes.

Remember that two of the first objects of competitions are to provide pleasure for competitors and to encourage others to take up training as a recreation. Please, I beseech you, try to look as if you were enjoying yourself! I am certain that the looks of grim determination and sheer agony on the faces of many competitors, not to mention some of the poor dogs, turn far more people against training than are won over by the competition itself.

After all, whether your dog does well or does badly in competitions he is still the same dog. You can still have the same enjoyment in training him, in taking him for walks and in doing all the other things which give so much pleasure to so many dogs and owners. If he wins in competitions he will add a thrill to your life, a thrill derived through the human desire to be 'top dog'.

I hope that this book may have helped some owners to

realize that satisfaction. My greatest hope, however, is that it has helped you, my reader, to have a more obedient dog than when you started – a dog that will give you more pleasure and which will derive more pleasure from you. And possibly neighbours who will derive greater pleasure from both you and your dog! If he does not win every time you compete in competition, does it really matter all that much?

Kennel Club Regulations
for tests for Obedience Classes
S(2)

1st January, 1985

1. Kennel Club Show Regulations shall where applicable and as amended or varied from time to time apply to Obedience Classes as follows:

Kennel Club Championship Show Regulations } to Championship Obedience Shows

Kennel Club Licence Show Regulations } to Licence Obedience Shows

Kennel Club Regulations for Sanction Shows } to Sanction Obedience Shows

2. A Show Society may schedule the following classes at a show. No variation to any test within a class may be made.

Classes may be placed in any order in the schedule but this order must be followed at the show except that a Society, by publication in the schedule, may reserve the right to vary the order of judging when the entry is known.

The maximum number of entries permitted in a Class for one Judge to judge shall be sixty. Except for Class C where Obedience Certificates are on offer, if this number is exceeded the Class shall be equally divided by a draw, each division to be judged separately. The prize money for each division shall be the same as that offered for the original Class. Where the entry for Class C exceeds sixty the number will be reduced to sixty by ballot which will be conducted by the Kennel Club when it conducts the ballot for the running order. No Judge shall judge more than sixty dogs in one day and if a Judge is appointed for two or more Classes the combined total of which exceeds sixty, a Reserve Judge will officiate. The Reserve Judge may enter dogs for competition at the Show and if not called upon to judge may compete. Show Societies should appoint sufficient judges for the expected entries.

Where a Class is divided, exhibitors entered for the Class shall be notified of all changes or alterations and no timed stay exercises are to be held earlier than those advertised for the original Class.

In Class C where Obedience Certificates are on offer one Judge only may be appointed for each sex. Judges must be present at all times the dogs are under test including the stay exercises.

3.a. In all the classes the handler may use the dog's name with a command or signal without penalty. Except in the Stay Tests and Distant Control, all tests shall

171

commence and finish with the dog sitting at the handler's side except in Beginners, Novice and Class A Recall Tests when the dog may be left in either the Sit or Down position at the handler's choice.

b. Food shall not be given to a dog in the ring.

c. In any test in which Judge's articles are used, none of them should be injurious to the dog, and they must be capable of being picked up by any breed entered in that test.

d. Spayed bitches and castrated dogs are permitted to compete in Obedience Classes.

e. No bitch in season shall be allowed to compete in Obedience Classes.

f. In all tests the points must be graduated.

g. Handlers may use only a slip chain or smooth collar on the dog when in the ring.

h. Every handler must wear a ring number prominently displayed when in the ring.

i. The Show Executive shall appoint a Chief Steward whose name must be announced in the schedule and who must not enter or work a dog at the Show. The Chief Steward alone shall be responsible for the control of any running order and for the smooth running of each class, and whose decision in such matters shall be personally conveyed to the Judge and shall be final.

j. The Show Executive shall ensure that 'Caller' Stewards are appointed for each class scheduled who must not work a dog at the Show.

k. A draw for the running order in Class C at Championship Shows must be made prior to the Show and exhibitors and Judges must be notified of the running order before the day of the Show. The Kennel Club will ballot for the running order for Championship Class C and Show Secretaries must forward lists of entries by recorded delivery or registered post to the Kennel Club for a ballot within 7 days after the closing of entries. Where a complete draw for the running order of classes other than Championship Class C is not made, Show Managements must ensure that at least 10 competitors/dogs are available, by means of a ballot, for judging in the first hour following the scheduled time for the commencement of judging of that class and these competitors must be notified prior to the Show. All competitors must personally report to the Ring Scoreboard Steward and book in within one hour of the scheduled time for the commencement of judging for the class. Those reporting late will be excluded from competition unless they have reported previously to the Chief Steward that they are actually working a dog entered in another Championship Class C or in the Stay Tests of another class. Where a complete running order is made, all competitors must be notified prior to the day of the Show and must book in on arrival at the Show. Published orders of running must be strictly adhered to.

Where timed stays will take place it must be announced in the schedule that they take priority over other tests. The times of such tests to be published at the Show and in the catalogue. In the case of Championship Class C, stays must not be judged before 12 noon.

Where Championship Class C competitors are required to compete in another Class at the Show, the Chief Steward will agree with the judges of these other classes that the judging of such competitors be re-arranged in the running order.

It is the responsibility of competitors to advise the Chief Steward of the clash of judging.

In all Scent Tests, dogs should compete in the same order as for previous tests, but the Judge may relax the running order where necessary. Scent tests must not be carried out during the main ring work but will take place as a separate test at the Judge's discretion.

l. Judging rings shall not in any circumstances contain less than 83 square metres (900 square feet) of clear floor space and shall be not less than 6 metres (20 feet) in width except that for Championship Class C the ring must contain not less than 148 square metres (1,600 square feet).

m. No person shall carry out punitive correction or harsh handling of a dog at any time whilst within the boundaries of the show.

n. Judges at Championship Shows

i. For Class C at Championship Shows Judges must have had at least five years' judging experience and must have judged at thirty Open Obedience Shows at which they must have judged Class C not less than 15 times. Judging experience of other classes must include at least 2 each of the following at Open or Championship Shows: Beginners, Novice, Class A and Class B.

ii. For all other classes, other than Class C, the Judge must have had at least three years' judging experience at twenty Open Obedience Shows and have judged Beginners, Novice, Class A and Class B each on 2 occasions at Open Shows.

o. Judges at Open Shows

On first appointment must satisfy the Show Committee that they have two years' experience judging at a lower level, have worked a dog in Licensed Obedience Shows and have acted as a Caller Steward or Marker Steward on six occasions at Licensed Shows.

p. A Judge of Class C must record in the judging book each dog awarded 290 points or more. The Show Secretary will record these in the official marked catalogue.

q. Any dog which is not presented for stay or scent exercises when called for testing, will be considered to have withdrawn from the class.

4. Imperfections in heeling between tests will not be judged but any physical disciplining of the dog by the handler in the ring, or any uncontrolled behaviour of the dog, such as snapping, unjustified barking, fouling the ring, or running out of the ring, even between tests, must be penalized by deducting points from the total score and the Judge may bar the dog from further competition in the class.

5.a. In all the following Definitions of Classes, First Prize wins in Limited and Sanction Show Obedience Classes and Open Shows confined to one breed will not count for entry in Open and Championship Show Obedience Classes. No dog is eligible to compete in Obedience Classes at Limited and Sanction Shows which has won an Obedience Certificate or obtained any award that counts towards the title of Obedience Champion or the equivalent thereof under the rules of any governing body recognized by the Kennel Club. Obedience Champions are eligible to compete only in Class C at Open and Championship Shows.

b. A dog may be entered in any two classes at a Show for which it is eligible with the exception of Championship Class C for which only dogs qualified may be entered. (Note the qualifications for Championship Class C and Obedience Warrant.)

Pre-Beginners

Pre-Beginners Classes may only be scheduled at Limited and Sanction Obedience Shows. If owner or handler or dog have won a first prize in any Class they may not compete in Pre-Beginners.

Handlers will not be penalized for encouragement or extra commands except in the Sit and Down tests. In these tests, at the discretion of the Judge, handlers may face their dogs. Judges or Stewards must not use the words 'last command' except in the Sit and Down tests.

1. Heel on Lead	15 points
2. Heel Free	20 points
3. Recall from sit or down position at handler's choice. Dog to be recalled by handler when stationary and facing the dog. Dog to return smartly to the handler, sit in front, go to heel — all on command of Judge or Steward to handler. Distance at discretion of Judge. Test commences when handler leaves dog	10 points
4. Sit one minute, handler in sight	10 points
5. Down two minutes, handler in sight	20 points
	Total 75 points

Beginners

If owner or handler or dog have won a total of two or more first prizes in the Beginners Class, they may not compete in Beginners. Winners of one first prize in any other Obedience Class are ineligible to compete in this Class.

Handlers will not be penalized for encouragement or extra commands except in the Sit and Down tests. In these tests, at the discretion of the Judge, handlers may face their dogs. Judges or Stewards must not use the words 'last command' except in the Sit and Down tests.

1. Heel on lead	15 points
2. Heel free	20 points
3. Recall from sit or down position at handler's choice. Dog to be recalled by handler when stationary and facing the dog. Dog to return smartly to handler, sit in front, go to heel — all on command of Judge or Steward to handler. Distance at discretion of judge. Test commences when handler leaves dog	10 points
4. Retrieve any article. Handlers may use their own article	25 points
5. Sit one minute, handler in sight	10 points
6. Down two minutes, handler in sight	20 points
	Total 100 points

Novice

For dogs that have not won two first prizes in Obedience Classes (Beginners Class excepted).

Handlers will not be penalized for encouragement or extra commands except in the Sit and Down tests. In these tests, at the discretion of the Judge, handlers may face their dogs. Judges or Stewards must not use the words 'last command' except in the Sit, Down and Stand tests.

1. Temperament Test. To take place immediately before heel on   10 points
lead. Dog to be on lead in the Stand position, handler to stand by
dog. Judge to approach quietly from the front and to run his
hand gently down the dog's back. Judge may talk quietly to dog
to reassure it. Any undue resentment, cringing, growling or
snapping to be penalized. This is not a stand for examination or
a stay test.   10 points
2. Heel on lead
3. Heel free   15 points
4. Recall from sit or down position at handler's choice. Dog to
be recalled by handler when stationary and facing the dog. Dog
to return smartly to handler, sit in front, go to heel — all on command of Judge or Steward to handler. Distance at discretion
of Judge. Test commences when handler leaves dog   10 points
5. Retrieve a dumb-bell. Handlers may use their own dumb-
bells   15 points
6. Stand one minute, handler in sight   10 points
7. Sit one minute, handler in sight   10 points
8. Down three minutes, handler in sight   20 points

Total 100 points

Class A
For dogs which have not won three first prizes in Classes A, B, and Open Class C in total.

Simultaneous command and signal will be permitted. Extra commands or signals must be penalized.

1. Heel on lead   15 points
2. Temperament Test. Will take place before Heel Free. Dog to
be in the stand position and off lead. Handler to stand beside
dog. Conditions as for Novice Temperament Test, except that
Test will commence with order 'last command' and end with
order 'test finished'. Extra commands will be penalized. This is
not a stand for examination or a stay test   10 points
3. Heel free   15 points
4. Recall from Sit or Down position at handler's choice. Dog to
be recalled to heel by handler, on command of Judge or Steward,
whilst handler is walking away from dog, both to continue forward until ordered to halt. The recall and halt points to be the
same for each dog and handler. Test commences following
handler's last command to dog.   15 points
5. Retrieve a dumb-bell. Handlers may use their own dumb-
bells   15 points
6. Stand two minutes, handler in sight   10 points
7. Sit two minutes, handler in sight.   10 points
8. Down five minutes, handler out of sight   30 points
9. Scent Discrimination, handler's scent on Judge's article. The
total number of articles shall not exceed ten, all of which
shall be clearly visible to the dog   30 points

Total 150 points

Class B
For dogs which have not won three first prizes in Class B and Open Class C in total.

One command, by word or signal, except in Test 2. Extra commands or signals must be penalized.

1. Heel Free. The dog shall be required to walk at heel free and shall also be tested at fast and slow pace. Each change of pace shall commence from the 'halt' position   30 points

2. Send Away, Drop and Recall. On command of Judge to handler, dog to be sent away in direction indicated by Judge. After the dog has been dropped, handler will call the dog to heel whilst walking where directed by Judge and both will continue forward until ordered to halt. No obstacle to be placed in path of dog. Simultaneous command and signal is permitted but as soon as the dog leaves the handler, the arm must be dropped. (N B an extra command may be simultaneous command and signal, but must be penalized.)   40 points

3. Retrieve any one article provided by the Judge but which must not be in any manner injurious to the dog (excluding food or glass). The article to be picked up easily by any breed of dog in that Class and to be clearly visible to the dog. A separate similar article to be used for each dog. Test commences following Judge or Steward's words 'last command' to handler   30 points

4. Stand two minutes, handler out of sight   15 points

5. Sit two minutes, handler out of sight   15 points

6. Down ten minutes, handler out of sight   40 points

7. Scent Discrimination. Handler's scent on article provided by Judge. A separate similar article to be used for each dog and the total number of articles shall not exceed ten, all of which shall be clearly visible to the dog and shall be similar to the article given to the handler. Judges must use a separate similar scent decoy or decoys for each dog. No points will be awarded if the article is given to the dog   30 points

Total 200 points

Class C
At Championship Shows: For dogs which have been placed on at least one occasion not lower than third in each class of Novice Class, Class A, Class B and have won Open Class C with not less than 290 marks on one occasion and have gained at least 290 marks in Open Class C on three further occasions under different Judges. Dogs which qualified for entry in Championship Class C prior to 1 May 1980 are also eligible.

At Limited and Sanction Shows: Open to all dogs except Obedience Certificate winners and dogs which have obtained any award that counts towards the title of Obedience Champion or the equivalent thereof under the rules of any governing body recognized by the Kennel Club.

One command, by word or signal, except in Test 2 where an extra command may be simultaneous command and signal. Extra commands or signals must be penalized.

1. Heel Work. The dog shall be required to walk at heel free, and also be tested at fast and slow pace. At some time during this test, at the discretion of the Judge, the dog shall be required whilst walking to heel at normal pace, to be left at the Stand, Sit and Down position in any order (the order to be the same for each dog) as and when directed by the Judge. The handler shall continue forward alone, without hesitation, and continue as directed by the Judge until reaching the dog when both shall continue forward together until halted. Heel work may include left about turns and figure-of-eight at normal and/or slow pace   60 points

2. Send Away, Drop and Recall as in Class B   40 points

3. Retrieve any one article provided by the Judge but which must not be in any manner injurious to the dog (excluding food or glass). The article to be picked up easily by any breed of dog in that Class and to be clearly visible to the dog. A separate similar article to be used for each dog. Test commences following Judge or Steward's 'last command' to handler   30 points

4. Distant Control. Dog to Sit, Stand and Down at a marked place not less than ten paces from handler, in any order on command from Judge to handler. Six instructions to be given in the same order for each dog. Excessive movement i.e. more than the length of the dog, in any direction by the dog, having regard to its size, will be penalized. The dog shall start the exercise with its front feet behind a designated point. No penalty for excessive movement in a forward direction shall be imposed until the back feet of the dog pass the designated point   50 points

5. Sit two minutes, handler out of sight   20 points

6. Down ten minutes, handler out of sight   50 points

7. Scent Discrimination. Judge's scent on a piece of marked cloth. Neutral and decoy cloths to be provided by the Show Executive. The Judge shall not place his cloth in the ring himself, but it shall be placed by a Steward. A separate similar piece to be used for each dog and the total number of separate similar pieces of cloth from which the dog shall discriminate shall not exceed ten. If a dog fetches or fouls a wrong article this must be replaced by a fresh article. At open-air shows all scent cloths must be adequately weighted to prevent them being blown about. The method of taking scent shall be at the handler's discretion but shall not require the Judge to place his hand on or lean towards the dog. A separate similar piece of cloth approximately 6 in. by 6 in. but not more than 10 in. by 10 in. shall be available to be used for giving each dog the scent. Judges should use a scent decoy or decoys   50 points

Total 300 points

6. The Kennel Club will offer an Obedience Certificate (Dog) and an Obedience Certificate (Bitch) for winners of first prizes in Class C Dog and Class C Bitch at a Championship Show, provided that the exhibits do not lose more than 10 points out of 300, and provided also that the classes are open to all breeds.

Judges must also award a Reserve Best of Sex provided that the exhibit has not lost more than 10 points out of 300.

7. The Kennel Club will offer at Crufts Dog Show each year the Kennel Club Obedience Championship—(Dog) and the Kennel Club Obedience Championship—(Bitch). A dog awarded one or more Obedience Certificates during the calendar year preceding Crufts Dog Show shall be entitled to compete.

The Tests for the Championships shall be those required for Class C in these Regulations. If the winning dog or bitch has lost more than 10 points out of 300, the Championship award shall be withheld.

8. As provided in Kennel Club Rule 4(c), the following dogs shall be entitled to be described as Obedience Champions and shall receive a Certificate to that effect from the Kennel Club:

a. The winners of the Kennel Club Obedience Championships.

b. A dog awarded three Obedience Certificates under three different Judges in accordance with these Regulations.

Explanatory Notes for Obedience Tests
(To be read in conjunction with Regulations S(2))

In all classes the dog should work in a happy natural manner and prime consideration should be given to judging the dog and handler as a team. The dog may be encouraged and praised except where specifically stated.

Instructions and commands to competitors may be made either by the Judge or the Steward by delegation.

In all tests the left side of a handler will be regarded as the 'working side' unless the handler suffers from a physical disability and has the Judge's permission to work the dog on the right-hand side.

To signal the completion of each test the handler will be given the command 'test finished'.

It is permissible for handlers to practise their dogs before going into the ring provided there is no punitive correction; this is similar to an athlete warming up before an event.

Timetable of Judging
To assist show executives the following guide timetable is issued:

Class C	8 dogs per hour
Class B	10 dogs per hour
Class A	12 dogs per hour
Novice	12 dogs per hour
Beginners	15 dogs per hour
Pre-beginners	18 dogs per hour

The dog should be led into the ring for judging with a collar and lead attached (unless otherwise directed) and should be at the handler's side. Competitors in Championship Class C who have lost more marks than would enable them to qualify with 290 marks at the conclusion of the judging may withdraw from the Class with the Judge's approval. This decision to withdraw is entirely at the discretion of the competitor and Judges must not compel such competitors to withdraw.

1. Heel on Lead
The dog should be sitting straight at the handler's side. On command the handler should walk briskly forward in a straight line with the dog at heel. The dog's

shoulder should be approximately level with and reasonably close to the handler's leg at all times when the handler is walking. The lead must be slack at all times. On the command 'left turn' or 'right turn' the handler should turn smartly at a right angle in the appropriate direction and the dog should keep its position at the handler's side. Unless otherwise directed, on the command 'about turn' the handler should turn about smartly through an angle of 180° to the right and walk in the opposite direction, the dog maintaining its position at the handler's side. On the command 'halt' the handler should halt immediately and the dog should sit straight at the handler's side. Throughout this test the handler may not touch the dog or make use of the lead without penalty.

2. Heel Free
This test should be carried out in a similar manner as for Heel on Lead except that the dog must be off the lead throughout the test.

'Left about turns' in heel work are only permissible in Classes B and C at the Judge's discretion.

3. Recall
See specific Class tests.

4. Retrieve a Dumb-Bell/Article
At the start of this exercise the dog should be sitting at the handler's side. On command the handler must throw the dumb-bell/article in the direction indicated. The dog should remain in the Sit position until the handler is ordered to send it to retrieve the dumb-bell/article. The dog should move out promptly at a smart pace to collect the dumb-bell/article cleanly. It should return with the dumb-bell/article at a smart pace and sit straight in front of the handler. On command the handler should take the dumb-bell/article from the dog. On further command the dog should be sent to heel. In Classes A, B and C the test commences on the order 'last command' to handler.

5.a. Sit/Stay
The Judge or Steward will direct handlers to positions in the ring. The command 'last command' will be given and handlers should then instantly give their final command to their dogs. Any further commands or signals to the dogs after this 'last command' will be penalized. Handlers will then be instructed to leave their dogs and walk to positions indicated until ordered to return to them. Dogs should remain at the Sit position throughout the test. This is a group test and all dogs must compete together, but where this is impracticable at an indoor show the Class may be equally divided but the judging for the groups must be consecutive.

b. Stand/Stay
This test should be carried out exactly as for the Sit/Stay, except that dogs will be left in the Stand position throughout the Test. This is a group test and all dogs must compete together, but where this is impracticable at an indoor show the Class may be equally divided but the judging for the groups must be consecutive.

c. Down/Stay
This test should be carried out exactly as for the Sit/Stay, except that dogs will be left in the Down position throughout the Test. This is a group test and all dogs

must compete together, but where this is impracticable at an indoor show the Class may be equally divided but the judging for the groups must be consecutive.

5. Scent Discrimination

A Steward will place the scented article amongst up to a maximum of nine other articles.

In a scent test if a dog brings in a wrong article or physically fouls any article (i.e. mouths it) this article will be replaced.

The dog should at this time be facing away from the articles. On command the handler should bring the dog to a point indicated, give the dog scent and stand upright before sending the dog to find and retrieve the appropriate article. The dog should find the article and complete the test as for the Retrieve test. In all tests, scent articles are to be placed at least 2 and not more than 4 feet apart. Limiting the time allowed for this test is at the Judge's discretion.

Class A – Handler's scent on article provided by the Judge.
This must not be given to the dog. In this test at least one article must be scented by someone other than the handler and must be similar for each dog. The remaining articles must be of a suitable variety in shape, size and substance.

Class B – Handler's scent on article provided by the Judge.
All articles must be separate and similar and must not be given to the dog.

Class C – Judge's scent on piece of marked cloth.
A decoy Steward should not handle a cloth for a period longer than the Judge.

Kennel Club Working Trial Regulations S(1)

10th August, 1982

1. **Management of Working Trials** – The management of a Working Trial shall be entrusted to a Working Trial Manager who shall be responsible for ensuring that the regulations are observed but he may not interfere with the Judges' decisions which shall be final.

The Working Trial Manager, appointed by the Committee of the Society holding the Trial, shall decide upon any matter not related to judging and not provided for in the Kennel Club Rules and Regulations for Working Trials and Obedience Classes and may call upon the Judge or Judges to assist with the decision which shall be final. The Working Trial Manager may not compete at the Trial and should be present throughout.

2. **Judges** – When a Judge, from ill-health or any other unexpected cause, is prevented from attending or finishing a meeting, the Working Trial Manager once the Trial has commenced shall have the power of deciding what action is to be taken.

3. **Schedule** – A Society holding a Working Trial must issue a schedule which is to be treated as a contract between the Society and the public and neither party is permitted to make any modification before the date of the Trial, except by permission of the Kennel Club, such alterations to be advertised in suitable publications where possible.

The schedule must contain:

a. The date and place of the Working Trial.

b. The latest date for applying for entry at the Trial. A separate official entry form which must be an exact copy of the wording of the specimen entry form issued by the Kennel Club.

c. The amounts of entry fees and any prize money.

d. The conditions of the draw for the order of running.

e. The conditions and qualifications for making entries and for intimating acceptance or refusal of entries.

f. An announcement that the Working Trial is held under Kennel Club Working Trial Rules and Regulations with such exceptions and conditions as the Committee of the Society may decide. Such exceptions and conditions must have received the approval of the General Committee of the Kennel Club prior to publication of the schedule.

g. The definition of each Stake, together with the qualification or limitations for entry in that Stake.

h. The names of Judges. An announcement that if the entries in the Companion Dog Stake exceed 20, a Judge may be appointed to judge the Group IV exercises and the competitors notified accordingly.

i. An announcement that except for Bloodhound Trials, dogs under the age of 18 months are not eligible for entry.

4. Assessing Weather Conditions – The Working Trial Manager and the Judges should assess the weather conditions and should they consider the weather unfit for holding the Trials the commencement may be postponed until such time as is considered necessary for the Trials to be abandoned and the entry fees returned.

5. Handling of Dogs by Owner or his Deputy – An owner or handler may handle the dog, but it must be one or the other; and once the dogs have commenced work an owner must not interfere with his dog if he has deputed another person to handle it.

6. Certification by Judge(s) – The Judge(s) shall certify on a form provided by the Kennel Club that in their opinion the Stake was held in accordance with the Schedule and Kennel Club Rules and Regulations.

7. Disqualification of Dogs – A dog shall be disqualified by the Judges and removed from the ground if in their opinion it is:

a. Unfit to compete by reason of sexual causes.

b. Suffering from any infectious or contagious disease.

c. Interfering with the safety or chance of winning of an opponent.

d. Of such temperament or is so much out of hand as to be a danger to the safety of any person or other animal.

e. Likely to cause cruelty to the dog if it continues in the Trial.

If a dog competes which has been exposed to the risk of any contagious or infectious disease during the period of six weeks prior to the Working Trial and/or if any dog shall be proved to be suffering at a Working Trial from any contagious or infectious disease, the owner thereof shall be liable to be dealt with under Rule 9 of the Kennel Club Rules for Working Trials and Obedience Classes.

8. Certificates – The Judge or Judges shall give certificates at a Championship Working Trial PD (Police Dog), TD (Tracking Dog), WD (Working Dog), UD (Utility Dog) and CD (Companion Dog) Stake to those dogs which have obtained 70% or more marks in each group of exercises in the Stake entered (provided that the dog has complied with any additional requirements for that Stake). The added qualification 'Excellent' shall be awarded should the dog also obtain 80% or more marks of the total for the Stake.

Societies may issue these Qualification Certificates in Championship Stakes to their own design, subject to the approval of the Kennel Club but they must contain the name and breed of the dog, the name of the owner, the title of the Society and date of the Trials, the qualification and marks awarded and the signatures of the Judge and Working Trial Manager.

The Judge or Judges at Open Working Trials run to these schedules shall give Certificates of Merit for those dogs whose marks would have gained them a qualification 'Excellent' at a Championship Working Trial, provided that the Certificate contains the following words: 'This Certificate does not entitle the dog named thereon to any qualification recognized by the Kennel Club except entry in appropriate Stakes at Championship Working Trials'. Such Certificates of Merit must contain the name and breed of the dog, the name of the owner, the title of the Society and date of the Trial, the Stake and the marks awarded (without reference to any qualification) and the signatures of the Judge(s) and Working Trial Manager.

9. Prizes – The winner of the Stake shall be the dog that has qualified with 70% or more marks in each group of the Stake and has obtained most marks. No dog that has not so qualified shall be placed in the prize list above a qualified dog. If no dog has qualified the dog with the highest number of marks may be awarded the prize. Judges are also empowered and instructed to withhold any prize or prizes if in their opinion the dogs competing do not show sufficient merit. Nothing in this Regulation shall apply to the award of 'Special' prizes.

10. Penalties for impugning the decisions of the Judges – If anyone taking part in the Trials openly impugns the decisions of the Judge or Judges, he is liable to be dealt with by the Committee under Rules 9 or 10 of the Kennel Club Rules for Working Trials and Obedience Classes.

11. Order of Running – The order of running tracks shall be determined by a draw and competitors notified accordingly prior to the day of the Trial.

12. Disqualification for Absence – The Working Trial Manager shall announce the specific time at which a dog or group of dogs may be called for any exercise or group of exercises. Each dog must be brought up at its proper time and in its proper turn without delay. If occasion demands the times and order may be changed at the discretion of the Working Trial Manager with the approval of the Judge or Judges, provided that no hardship is thereby caused to any competitor. If absent when called, the dog shall be liable to be disqualified by the Judge or Judges.

13. Method of Working – The Judge or Judges in consultation with the Working Trial Manager may arrange for dogs to be working singly or together in any numbers. All dogs entered in a Stake shall be tested as far as possible under similar conditions.

14. Regulations Regarding Handling
a. A person handling a dog may speak, whistle or work it by hand signals as he wishes, but he can be called to order by the Judge or Judges for making unnecessary noise, and if he persists in doing so the Judge or Judges can disqualify the dog.
b. No person shall carry out punitive correction or harsh handling of a dog.

15. Awards – All awards made by the Judge or Judges at a Working Trial shall be in accordance with the agreed scale of points approved by the General Committee of the Kennel Club. Equal awards for any of the prizes offered at a Working Trial are prohibited.

16. Notification of Awards – The Secretary of a Working Trial shall send (within 7 days of the Trial) the Judges' certification and two marked catalogues to the Kennel Club indicating the prize winners and those dogs to which the Judges have awarded Certificates.

17. Entry Forms – Entry Forms must be in accordance with the approved forms which must be issued by the Secretary of the Working Trial, and all entries must be made thereon and not otherwise, and entirely in ink; only one person shall enter on one form. All such entry forms must be preserved by the Committee of a Working Trial meeting for at least twelve months from the last day of the trial.

18. Refusal of Entries – The Committee of any Meeting may reserve to themselves the right of refusing any entries on reasonable grounds.

19. Objections to Dogs – An objection to a dog must be made to the Secretary in writing at any time within twenty-one days of the last day of the meeting upon the objector lodging with the Secretary the sum of £5.00. The deposit may be returned after the General Committee of the Kennel Club has considered the objection. Should any objection be made other than under Regulation 7(a) to 7(e) the dog should be allowed to compete and a full report made to the Kennel Club.

When an objection is lodged the Secretary of the Society must send to the Kennel Club:

a. A copy of the objection.
b. The name and address of the objector.
c. The name and address of the owner of the dog.
d. All relevant evidence.

The objection will then be dealt with by the General Committee of the Kennel Club whose decision shall be final.

No objection shall be invalidated solely on the grounds that it was incorrectly lodged.

If the dog objected to be disqualified, the prize to which it would otherwise have been entitled shall be forfeited, and the dog or dogs next in order of merit shall move up and take the prize or prizes.

No spectator, not being the owner of a dog competing, or his accredited representative has the right to lodge any objection to a dog or to any action taken at the meeting unless he be a member of the Committee of the Society or of the General Committee of the Kennel Club or a Steward. Any objection so lodged will be disregarded.

20. Withdrawal of dogs from Competition – No dog entered for competition and actually at the meeting, may be withdrawn from competition without notice to the Working Trials Manager. No dog shall compulsorily be withdrawn from a Stake by reason of the fact that it has obtained less than 70% of the marks in any one group.

21. Failure to Participate in Any Exercise – Failure to participate in any exercise in a group in any Stake shall result in failure to qualify in that group.

22. The Working Trials and Obedience Committee shall issue an Appendix to the Schedule of Exercises and Points, 'Description of Exercises and Guidance for Judges and Competitors at Working Trials', which they may from time to time alter and in respect of which notice shall be given in the Kennel Gazette.

23. Working Trials for Bloodhounds shall be exempt from Working Trial Regulations 8, 9, 14(a), 15 and 21 and the Definitions of Stakes and Schedule of Exercises and Points. Until further notice the schedule of each Bloodhound Working Trial shall be submitted to the Kennel Club for approval before publication in accordance with the provision of Rule 3 of the Kennel Club Rules for Working Trials and Obedience Classes.

Definitions of Stakes

When entering for Championship or Open Working Trials, wins at Members Working Trials will not count.

No dog entered in PD or TD Stakes shall be eligible to enter in any other Stake at the meeting.

All Police dogs shall be considered qualified for entry in WD Championship Stakes if they hold the Regional Police Dog qualification 'Excellent', provided that such entries are countersigned by the Senior Police Officer I/C when such entries are made. Dogs holding this qualification are not eligible for entry in CD or UD Open or Championship Stakes, nor in WD Open Stakes.

No Working Trial Stake shall be limited to less than 30 dogs. If a limit is imposed on entries in any Stake, it shall be carried out by ballot after the date of closing of entries. Championship TD or PD Stakes shall not be limited to numbers in any way.

Open Working Trial

Companion Dog (CD) Stake – For dogs which have not qualified CD Ex or UD Ex or won three or more first prizes in CD or any prize in UD Stakes, WD Stakes, PD or TD Stakes at Open or Championship Working Trials.

Utility Dog (UD) Stake – For dogs which have not been awarded a Certificate of Merit in UD, WD, PD or TD Stakes.

Working Dog (WD) Stake – For dogs which have been awarded a Certificate of Merit in UD Stakes but not in WD, PD or TD Stakes.

Tracking Dog (TD) Stake – For dogs which have been awarded a Certificate of Merit in WD Stakes but not more than two Certificates of Merit in TD Stakes.

Police Dog (PD) Stake – For dogs which have been awarded a Certificate of Merit in WD Stakes but not in PD Stakes.

Championship Working Trial

Companion Dog (CD) Stake – For dogs which have not won three or more first prizes in CD Stakes or any prize in any other Stake at Championship Working Trials.

Utility Dog (UD) Stake – For dogs which have won a Certificate of Merit in an Open UD Stake. A dog is not eligible for entry in this Stake if it has been entered in the WD Stake on the same day.

Working Dog (WD) Stake – For dogs which have qualified UD Ex and have won a Certificate of Merit in Open WD Stakes.

Tracking Dog (TD) Stake – For dogs which have been awarded two Certificates of Merit in Open TD Stakes and have qualified WD Ex at two Championship Working Trials.

Police Dog (PD) Stake – For dogs which have qualified WD Ex.

Members Working Trial

This is restricted to the members of the Society holding the Working Trial and eligibility for Stakes is as for Open Working Trials.

Judges at Championship Working Trials

For CD Stake: Must have judged at least two Open Working Trials and have as a handler qualified a dog 'Excellent' in a Championship CD Stake.

For UD Stake: Must have judged UD or WD Stakes at two Open Trials, have judged CD Stakes at a Championship Trial and have as a handler qualified a dog 'Excellent' in a Championship WD Stake.

For WD Stake: Must have judged UD or WD Stakes at two Open Trials, UD Stake at a Championship Trial and have as a handler qualified a dog 'Excellent' in a Championship WD Stake.

For PD Stake and TD Stake: Must have judged at two Open Trials, WD Stake at a Championship Trial and qualified a dog 'Excellent' in the Stake for which he was nominated to judge. There must be an interval of not less than six calendar months between appointments of the same judge for Championship TD and/or PD Stakes.

Note: Service and Police judges are eligible to judge UD Stake at a Championship Trial provided they have qualified a dog WD 'Excellent'. They must qualify for approval for other Stakes as above, except that those who have judged all parts at Regional or National Police Dog Trials will not have to qualify as a civilian handler.

Kennel Club Working Trial Championships

a. The Kennel Club Working Trial Championships at which Police Dog (PD) and Tracking Dog (TD) Stakes shall be scheduled are held annually.

b. The responsibility for organizing the Championships each year will normally be delegated to a Working Trial Society approved to hold Championship Working Trials, such Society to be selected by the Working Trials and Obedience Committee from applications submitted by Societies. No Society to stage the event two years in succession.

c. The Secretary of the Kennel Club will unless otherwise specified be the Working Trial Secretary for the event, the Society scheduling the Championships appointing a Trial Manager.

d. The following shall be the method of selection of judges for the Championships:
Nominated by Working Trials Societies which have been granted Championship Working Trial status for ballotting by Working Trial Council, final selection by the Working Trials and Obedience Committee.

e. Dogs eligible for entry in the Championships qualify as follows:
    i. TD Championship: A dog must have been placed 1st in Championship TD Stake and qualified 'Excellent' in the Stake during the period 1 October – 30 September preceding the Championships.
    ii. PD Championship: A dog must have been placed 1st in Championship

PD Stake and qualified 'Excellent' in the Stake during the period 1 October – 30 September preceding the Championships.

iii. Dogs which qualify as above in both PD and TD Championship Stakes are permitted to be entered in either or both Championship Stakes.

iv. The winners of the previous year's Championship Stakes qualify automatically.

v. No other dogs are eligible for entry in the Championships except by special permission of the General Committee of the Kennel Club.

f. The Championships will normally be held during the third weekend in October each year.

g. The winner of each Stake in the Championships is entitled to the description of Working Trial Champion provided it qualifies 'Excellent'.

h. The Working Trial Society selected to hold the Championships is allowed to forego one Open Working Trial during the same year.

Schedule of exercises and points

Companion Dog (CD) Stake

	Marks	Group Total	Minimum Group Qualifying Mark
Group I Control			
1. Heel on leash	5		
2. Heel free	10		
3. Recall to handler	5		
4. Sending the dog away	10	30	21
Group II Stays			
5. Sit (2 minutes)	10		
6. Down (10 minutes)	10	20	14
Group III Agility			
7. Scale (3) Stay (2) Recall (5)	10		
8. Clear jump	5		
9. Long jump	5	20	14
Group IV Retrieving and Nosework			
10. Retrieve a dumb-bell	10		
11. Elementary search	20	30	21
Totals	100	100	70

Utility Dog (UD) Stake

	Marks	Group Total	Minimum Group Qualifying Mark
Group I Control			
1. Heel free	5		
2. Sending the dog away	10		

3. Retrieve a dumb-bell	5		
4. Down (10 minutes)	10		
5. Steadiness to gunshot	5	35	25
Group II Agility			
6. Scale (3) Stay (2) Recall (5)	10		
7. Clear jump	5		
8. Long jump	5	20	14
Group III Nosework			
9. Search	35		
10. Track (95) Article (15)	110	145	102
Totals	200	200	141

Working Dog (WD) Stake

	Marks	Group Total	Minimum Group Qualifying Mark
Group I Control			
1. Heel free	5		
2. Sending the dog away	10		
3. Retrieve a dumb-bell	5		
4. Down (10 minutes)	10		
5. Steadiness to gunshot	5	35	25
Group II Agility			
6. Scale (3) Stay (2) Recall (5)	10		
7. Clear jump	5		
8. Long jump	5	20	14
Group III Nosework			
9. Search	35		
10. Track (90) Articles (10+10=20)	110	145	102
Totals	200	200	141

Tracking Dog (TD) Stake

	Marks	Group Total	Minimum Group Qualifying Mark
Group I Control			
1. Heel free	5		
2. Send away and directional control	10		
3. Speak on command	5		
4. Down (10 minutes)	10		
5. Steadiness to gunshot	5	35	25
Group II Agility			
6. Scale (3) Stay (2) Recall (5)	10		
7. Clear jump	5		
8. Long jump	5	20	14

Group III Nosework

		Marks		
9.	Search	35		
10.	Track (100) Articles (10+10+10=30)	130	165	116
	Totals	220	220	155

Police Dog (PD) Stake

		Marks	Group Total	Minimum Group Qualifying Mark
Group I Control				
1.	Heel Free	5		
2.	Send away and directional control	10		
3.	Speak on command	5		
4.	Down (10 minutes)	10		
5.	Steadiness to gunshot	5	35	25
Group II Agility				
6.	Scale (3) Stay (2) Recall (5)	10		
7.	Clear jump	5		
8.	Long jump	5	20	14
Group III Nosework				
9.	Search	35		
10.	Track (60) Articles (10+10=20)	80	115	80
Group IV Patrol				
11.	Quartering the ground	45		
12.	Test of courage	20		
13.	Search and escort	25		
14a.	Recall from criminal	30		
14b.	Pursuit and detention of criminal	30	150	105
	Totals	320	320	224

Description of Exercises and Guidance for Judges and Competitors at Working Trials

A. Method of Handling – Although implicit obedience to all orders is necessary, dogs and handlers must operate in as free and natural a manner as possible. Excessive formalism may be penalized, particularly if, in the opinion of the Judge, it detracts from the ability of the dog to exercise its senses in relation to all that is happening in the vicinity. Persistent barking, whining etc. in any exercise other than location of articles, person or speak on command should be penalized. Food may not be given to the dog by the handler whilst being tested.

B. Heel Work – The Judge should test the ability of the dog to keep his shoulder reasonably close to the left knee of the handler who should walk smartly in his natural manner at normal, fast and slow paces through turns and among and around persons and obstacles. The halt, with the dog sitting to heel and a 'figure of eight' may be included at any stage.

Any act, signal or command or jerking of the leash which in the opinion of the Judge has given the dog unfair assistance shall be penalized.

C. Sit (2 minutes) – Dogs may be tested individually or in a group or groups. The Judge or Stewards will give the command 'last command' and handlers should then instantly give their final commands to the dogs. Any further commands or signals to the dogs will be penalized. Handlers will then be instructed to leave their dogs and proceed to positions indicated by the Judge or Steward until ordered to return to them. Where possible, such positions should be out of sight of the dogs but bearing in mind the short duration of the exercise this may not be practical. Dogs must remain in the sit position throughout the test until the Judge or Steward indicates that the test has finished. Minor movements must be penalized. The Judge may use his discretion should interference by another dog cause the dog to move.

D. Down (10 minutes) – Handlers must be out of sight of the dogs who may be tested individually or in a group or groups. The Judge or Steward will give the command 'last command' and handlers should then instantly give their final commands to their dogs. Any further commands or signals to the dogs will be penalized. Handlers will then be instructed to leave their dogs and proceed to positions indicated by the Judge or Steward until ordered to return to them. Dogs must remain in the 'Down' position throughout the test until the Judge or Steward indicates that the test has finished. No dog will be awarded any marks that sits, stands or crawls more than its approximate body length in any direction. Minor movements must be penalized. The Judge may use his discretion should interference by another dog cause a dog to move. The Judge may test the dog by using distractions but may not call it by name.

E. Recall to Handler – The dog should be recalled from the 'Down' or 'Sit' position. The handler being a reasonable distance from the dog at the discretion of the Judge. The dog should return at a smart pace and sit in front of the handler, afterwards going smartly to heel on command or signal. Handler to await command of the Judge or Stewards.

F. Retrieve a Dumb-Bell – The dog should not move forward to retrieve nor deliver to hand on return until ordered by the handler on the Judge or Steward's instructions. The Retrieve should be executed at a smart pace without mouthing or playing with the object. After delivery the handler will send his dog to heel on the instructions of the Judge or Steward.

G. Send Away and Directional Control – The minimum distance that the Judge shall set for the Send Away shall be 20 yards for the CD Stake and 50 yards for all other Stakes. The TD and PD Stakes shall also include a redirection of a minimum of 50 yards. When the dog has reached the designated point or the Judge is satisfied that after a reasonable time the handler cannot improve the position of the dog by any further commands the dog should be stopped in either the stand, sit or down position at the discretion of the handler. At this point in the TD or PD Stakes the Judge or Steward shall instruct the handler to redirect his dog. In all Stakes, whilst the Judge should take into account the number of commands used during the exercise, importance should be placed upon the handler's ability to direct his dog to the place indicated.

H. Steadiness to Gunshot – The most appropriate occasion for testing this exercise would be in open country. The dog may be either walking at heel free or be away from the handler who must be permitted to remain within controlling distance whilst the gun is fired. Any sign of fear, aggressiveness or barking must be penalized. This test shall not be carried out without prior warning, or incorporated in any other test. The Judge will not provoke excitement by excessive display of the gun, nor shall the gun be pointed at the dog.

1. Speak on Command – The Judge will control the position of the handler in relation to the dog and may require the handler to work the dog walking at heel. If the dog is not required to walk at heel, the handler may at his discretion place the dog in the stand, sit or down. The dog will be ordered to speak and cease speaking on command of the Judge or Steward who may then instruct the handler to make the dog speak again. Speaking should be sustained by the dog whilst required with the minimum of commands and/or signals. Continuous and/or excessive incitements to speak shall be severely penalized. This test should not be incorporated with any other test.

J. Agility – No part of the scale or clear or long jump equipment to be traversed by a dog shall be less than three feet wide nor be in any way injurious to the dog. The tests shall be followed in a sequence agreed by the Judge and will commence with the Scale. The Scale should be a vertical wall of wooden planks and may have affixed on both sides three slats evenly distributed in the top half of the jump. The top surface of the Scale may be lightly padded. The handler should approach the Scale at a walking pace and halt four to nine feet in front of it and in his own time order the dog to scale. On reaching the other side the dog should be ordered to stay in the stand, sit or down position, the handler having previously nominated such a position to the Judge. The Judge should ensure that the dog will stay steady and may indicate to the handler where he should stand in relation to his dog and the Scale before ordering the dog to be recalled over the Scale. A dog which fails to go over the Scale at the second attempt shall be excluded from the stay and recall over the Scale. Failure in the recall over the Scale does not disqualify from marks previously gained.

The handler may either approach the clear and long lumps with the dog or send it forward or stand by the jumps and call the dog up to jump. At no time should the handler proceed beyond any part of the jumps before they have been traversed by the dog. Once the dog has cleared the obstacle he should remain on the other side under control until joined by the handler. The clear jump should be so constructed that it will be obvious if the dog has exerted more than slight pressure upon it. The rigid top bar may be fixed or rest in cups and the space below may be filled in but the filling should not project above the bottom of the top bar. Appreciable pressure exerted by the dog on the clear jump shall be considered to be a failure. Casual fouling with fore or hind legs will be penalized at the discretion of the Judge. Failure or refusal at any of the three types of jump may be followed by a second attempt and any one such failure shall be penalized by at least 50% of the marks allotted to that part of the exercise in which the dog is given a second attempt.

Jumping heights and lengths:
Companion Dog (CD) Stake and Utility Dog (UD) Stake
a. Scale

Dogs not exceeding 10 in. at shoulder	3 ft.
Dogs not exceeding 15 in. at shoulder	4 ft.
Dogs exceeding 15 in. at shoulder	6 ft.

b. Clear Jump

Dogs not exceeding 10 in. at shoulder	1 ft. 6 in.

Dogs not exceeding 15 in. at shoulder   2 ft.
Dogs exceeding 15 in. at shoulder   3 ft.
c. Long Jump
Dogs not exceeding 10 in. at shoulder   4 ft.
Dogs not exceeding 15 in. at shoulder   6 ft.
Dogs exceeding 15 in. at shoulder   9 ft.

Working Dog (WD) Stake, Tracking Dog (TD) Stake and Police Dog (PD) Stake

a. Scale   6 ft.
b. Clear Jump   3 ft.
c. Long Jump   9 ft.

K. Search – The Companion Dog (CD) Stake Search shall contain three articles and all other Stakes shall contain four articles. In all Stakes fresh articles must be placed for each dog who must recover a minimum of two articles to qualify. As a guide the articles should be similar in size to a six inch nail or a match box, but the Judge should choose articles in relation to the nature of the ground and the Stake which he is judging. The time allotted shall be four minutes in the CD Stake and five minutes in all other Stakes. The articles should be well handled and placed by a Steward who shall foil the ground by walking in varying directions over the area. Each competitor shall have a separate piece of land.

The CD Stake search area shall be 15 yards square, all other Stakes being 25 yards square and shall be clearly defined by a marker peg at each corner. The handler may work his dog from any position outside the area, provided that he does not enter it.

In the CD Stake a maximum five marks should be allotted for each article and a maximum five marks for style and control. In all other Stakes a maximum seven marks should be allotted for each article and a maximum seven marks for style and control.

L. Track – The track should be plotted on the ground to be used for the nosework by Stewards previous to the day of commencement of the Trials. An area of ground which has had a track laid over it must not have another track laid over it until the following day. The track shall be single line and may include turns. The articles should be in keeping with the nature of the ground. There shall be a marker left by the tracklayer to indicate the start of the track. In the UD Stake a second marker should be left not more than 30 yards from the start to indicate the direction of the first leg.

Unless the Judge considers the dog to have lost the track beyond recovery or has run out of the time allotted for the completion of the track a handler may recast his dog at his discretion. The Judge should not at any time indicate to the handler where he should recast his dog except in exceptional circumstances.

The track shall be approximately half a mile long and should be laid as far as possible by a stranger to the dog. The article(s) should be well scented. When the judging is in progress the tracklayer shall be present at the side of the Judge to indicate the exact line of the track and the position of the articles.

The UD Stake track shall be not less than half an hour old and shall include one article at the end, recovery of the article not being a requirement for qualification.

The WD and PD Stake tracks shall be not less than one and a half hours old and shall include two articles one of which must be recovered to qualify.

The TD Stake track shall be not less than three hours old and shall include three articles two of which must be recovered to qualify.

In all Stakes the last article shall indicate the end of the track. No two articles should be laid together.

A spare track additional to requirements should be laid but the opportunity to run a new track should be given only in exceptional circumstances.

The area used for Tracking is out of bounds to all competitors for practice Tracks and exercise from the time of the first track and any competitor found contravening this instruction is liable to be disqualified by the Judge and/or Stewards from participating in the Trial in accordance with the provision of Regulation No. 7(c).

The dog must be worked on a harness and tracking line.

M. Quartering the Ground– The missing person or criminal should be protected to the minimum extent consistent with safety. He should remain motionless out of sight of the handler, but should be accessible on investigation to a dog which has winded him.

The Judge should satisfy himself that the dog has found the person and has given warning spontaneously and emphatically without being directed by the handler. Once the person has been detected and the dog has given voice, he may offer meat or other food which should be refused by the dog. If the dog ignores the food he may throw it on the ground in front of the dog. A dog which bites the person or criminal must be severely penalized.

N. Test of Courage– This is a test of courage rather than of control. Dogs will not be heavily penalized in this test for lack of control. Handlers must be prepared to have the dog tested when on the lead by an unprotected Judge or Steward, and/or when off the lead by a protected Steward. The method of testing will be at the discretion of the Judge.

O. Search and Escort– The criminal will be searched by the handler with the dog off the lead at the sit, stand or down. The Judge will assess whether the dog is well placed tactically and ready to defend if called to do so.

The handler will then be told to escort the prisoner(s) at least 30 yards in a certain direction, he will give at least one turn on the direction of the Judge. During the exercise the criminal will turn and attempt to overcome the handler. The dog may defend spontaneously or on command and must release the criminal at once both when he stands still or when the handler calls him off. The handler should be questioned as to his tactics in positioning the dog in both search and escort.

P. Recall from Criminal (Exercise 14(a)) – The criminal, protected to the minimum extent consistent with safety, will be introduced to the handler whose dog will be free at heel. After an unheated conversation the criminal will run away. At a reasonable distance the handler will be ordered to send his dog. When the dog is approximately halfway between handler and the criminal he will be ordered to be recalled. The recall may be by whistle or voice. The criminal should continue running until the dog returns or closes. If the dog continues to run alongside the criminal the criminal should run a further ten or dozen paces to indicate this.

Q. Pursuit and Detention of Criminal (Exercise 14(b)) – The criminal (a different one for choice) and handler should be introduced as above, and the dog sent forward under the same conditions. The criminal must continue to attempt to escape and, if possible, should do so through some exit or in some vehicle once the dog has had a chance to catch up with him. The dog must be regarded as having succeeded if it clearly prevents the criminal from continuing his line of flight, either by holding him by the arm, knocking him over or close circling him till he becomes giddy. If the dog fails to make a convincing attempt to detain the criminal, it shall lose any marks that it may have obtained under exercise 14(a) or alternatively, it shall not be tested on exercise 14(a) if that follows exercise 14(b).

Kennel Club Regulations for Working Trial Rallies and Matches S(I) (a)

10th August, 1982

1. Registered Clubs, Societies and Dog Training Clubs only may hold Working Trial Rallies and Matches.

2. A Club may not hold more than twelve Working Trial Rallies and Matches per annum. In the case of Clubs which have Registered Branches, each Branch may hold not more than 12 Working Trial Matches and Rallies per annum. A Working Trial Rally or Match may be an inter-Club competition between Associations, Clubs, Societies or Branches of Clubs. No exercise at a Rally or Match shall vary from those contained in the Kennel Club Working Trial Regulations.

3. Applications for permission to hold Working Trial Rallies and Matches must be made in the form of a letter to the Secretary of the Kennel Club at least fourteen days before the date of the proposed Working Trial Rally or Match. A fee of £1.15 must be forwarded with each application.

4. A dog must, at the time of competition, be registered at the Kennel Club. The Committee of the organizing Club may reserve the right to refuse any entry on reasonable grounds. Exhibits must be the property of members of one of the Associations, Clubs, Societies or Branches competing in the Working Trial Rally or Match.

5. Puppies under six calendar months of age are not eligible for competition at Working Trial Rallies and Matches.

6. If a dog competes which has been exposed to the risk of any contagious or infectious disease during the period of six weeks prior to the Working Trial Rally or Match and/or if any dog shall be proved to be suffering at Working Trial Rallies or Matches from any contagious or infectious disease, the owner thereof shall be liable to be dealt with under Kennel Club Rule 17.

7. Not more than 52 dogs may compete at a meeting.

8. Prize cards, diplomas or other printed awards may be awarded at Working Trial Rallies or Matches provided such awards are white and clearly overprinted 'WORKING TRIAL RALLY' or 'WORKING TRIAL MATCH'.

9. Not more than 5 Special Prizes shall be awarded at Working Trial Rallies or Matches.

10. The organizing Club shall keep a list of the names and addresses of all competing dogs with awards and the names and addresses of their owners for a period of 12 months from the date of the Working Trial Rally or Match.

11. Fraudulent or Discreditable Conduct at Working Trial Rallies or Matches to be Reported:
The Executive of the organizing Club of a Working Trial Match or Rally must immediately report to the Secretary of the Kennel Club any case of alleged fraudulent or discreditable conduct, or any default or omission at or in connection with the Working Trial Match or Rally which may come under its notice, and at the same time forward to the Secretary of the Kennel Club all documents and information in connection therewith, which may be in its possession or power. Where fraudulent or discreditable conduct is alleged at a Working Trial Rally or Match in Scotland, the Executive of the organizing Club must make such report in the first instance to the Secretary of the Scottish Kennel Club.

Kennel Club Regulations for Agility Tests S(5)

21st May, 1986

1.   Registered Clubs, Societies, Dog Training Clubs, Kennel Club Licensed Shows and other organisations approved by the Kennel Club may hold Agility Tests. The Kennel Club reserves the right to refuse any application for a licence. Exemption Shows may not hold Agility Tests, however, they may be held in conjunction with Exemption Shows provided they are organised by a Registered Society and a separate Agility licence is issued.

2.   Application for permission to hold Agility Tests must be made in the form of a letter to the Secretary of the Kennel Club at least six months before the date of the proposed event. A fee of £5.00 must be forwarded with the application together with a schedule for the event which must contain:
a.   The date, place and time of the event.
b.   A separate official entry form which must be an exact copy of wording of the specimen entry form issued by the Kennel Club.
c.   The amounts of entry fees and any prize money.
d.   The method by which the judge will mark the tests.
e.   The qualifications for entry in the tests scheduled.
f.   An announcement that the Tests are held under Kennel Club Regulations for Agility Tests.
g.   An announcement that the organising committee reserve the right to refuse any entry.
h.   The names of the judges.

3.   A dog must, at the time of the competition be registered at the Kennel Club. The Committee of the organising Club may reserve the right to refuse entry.

4.   Puppies under 12 calendar months of age and bitches in season are not eligible for competition in Agility Tests.

5.   If a dog competes which has been exposed to the risk of any contagious or infectious disease during the period of six weeks prior to the Agility Tests and/or if any dog shall be proved to be suffering at Agility Tests from any contagious or infectious disease, the owner thereof shall be liable to be dealt with under Kennel Club Rule 17.

6.   The organising Club shall keep a list of the names of all competing dogs with awards and the names and addresses of their owners for a period of twelve months from the date of the Agility Tests.

7.   A judge at an Agility Test cannot compete at that event on the same day.

8.   Fraudulent or Discreditable Conduct at Agility Tests to be Reported:
     The Executive of the organising Club of an Agility Test must immediately report to the Secretary of the Kennel Club any case of alleged fraudulent or discreditable conduct, any default or omission at or in connection with the Agility Test which may come under its notice, and at the same time forward to the Secretary of the Kennel Club all documents and information in connection therewith, which may be in its possession or power.
     Agility Tests are considered to be a 'fun' type competition designed for spectator appeal. However, competitors are reminded that they are subject to other Kennel Club Rules and Regulations where applicable.

9.   Delegated Powers of the Scottish Kennel Club. For the purposes of these Regulations, all powers of the General Committee relative to shows held in Scotland and licensed by the Scottish Kennel Club are delegated to the Executive Council of the Scottish Kennel Club. Applications for licences and queries, objections and allegations of fraudulent or discreditable conduct relative to Shows licensed by the Scottish Kennel Club, are to be made to the Secretary General of the Scottish Kennel Club, 6b Forres Street, Edinburgh EH3 6BJ.

Schedule of Tests

Agility Tests – Courses and Obstacles
The following obstacles meet with the approval of the Committee of the Kennel Club but organisers may submit others for approval if desired. No practice is to be allowed on the course.

1.   *Test Area.* The test area must measure not less than 40 yards × 30 yards and have a non-slip surface.

2.   *Course.* A minimum of ten and a maximum of 18 comprise a test course.

3.   *Obstacles.*
a.   *Hurdle:* Height: 2 ft. 6 in. maximum. Width: 4 ft. 0 in. minimum.
b.   *Dog Walk:* Height: 4 ft. 0 in. minimum, 4 ft. 6 in. maximum. Walk plank width: 8 in. minimum, 12 in. maximum. Length: 12 ft. 0 in. minimum, 14 ft. 0 in. maximum. Ramps to have anti-slip slats at intervals and to be firmly fixed to top plank.
c.   *Hoop:* Aperture diameter: 1 ft. 3 in. minimum. Aperture centre from ground: 3 ft. 0 in. maximum.
d.   *Brush Fence:* Dimensions as for hurdle.
e.   *Table:* Surface: 3 ft. 0 in. square minimum. Height: 3 ft. 0 in. maximum. To be of stable construction with non-slip surface.
f.   *Collapsible Tunnel:* Diameter: 2 ft. 0 in. minimum, 2 ft. 6 in. maximum. Length: 12 ft. 0 in. Circular of non-rigid material construction with entrance of rigid construction and fixed or weighted to the ground.
g.   *'A' ramp:* Length: 3 yards minimum, 3½ yards maximum. Width: 3 ft. 0 in. Height of apex from ground: 6 ft. 3 in. Two ramps hinged at apex. Surface of

ramps slatted at intervals.

h.   *Weaving Poles:* Number: 6 minimum, 12 maximum. Distance apart: 2 ft. 0 in. maximum.

i.   *Pipe Tunnel:* Diameter: 2 ft. minimum. Length: 10 ft. 0 in. minimum.

j.   *See-Saw:* Width: 8 in. minimum, 12 in. maximum. Length: 12 ft. 0 in. minimum, 14 ft. 0 in. maximum. Height of central bracket from ground: 2 ft. 3 in. maximum. A plank firmly mounted on central bracket.

k.   *Long-jump:* Length: 5 ft. maximum. Width: 4 ft. minimum. Height: 1 ft. maximum.

l.   *Pause Box:* Defined area: 4 ft. × 4 ft.

Marking

Standard Marking

5 faults for each failure to negotiate any obstacle correctly.

Failure to correctly complete the course – disqualified.

Other marking

Any form of marking other than 'Standard' must be stated in the schedule.

INDEX